Portraits of Jesus
in the Gospel of John

Portraits of Jesus
in the Gospel of John

ROBERT P. LIGHTNER

Resource *Publications*

An imprint of **Wipf and Stock Publishers**
199 West 8th Avenue • Eugene OR 97401

PORTRAITS OF JESUS IN THE GOSPEL OF JOHN

ISBN 10: 1-59752-878-1
ISBN 13: 978-1-59752-878-8

Manufactured in the U.S.A.

*To my brothers, Harold, Kenneth, and Richard,
and in memory of my sister, Lucille,
all of whom have trusted Jesus as their personal Savior.*

Contents

Introduction

WINSTON CHURCHILL, the famous defender of the British Empire, had a most fascinating and amazing career. He was 65 years old when he was called upon to become England's protector. Throughout his political life he demonstrated great and brilliant leadership. History will remember him as the one largely responsible for saving his nation from Nazi take-over. This man might be called England's savior.

Jesus of Nazareth, the very Son of God came to earth to be the world's Savior, not just England's. He was man, but more than man. As the God-Man, He, unlike all of us, was not born into the world dying. No, He was born of woman that He might die as a Substitute for the world's sinners.

One of Jesus' apostles whose name is John was especially close to Jesus during the three years of Jesus' public life and ministry. In the apostle's book called the Gospel of John, he paints what I call a number of portraits of Jesus. We will look seriously at 29 of them in this book.

John was Jesus' beloved disciple. He was one of the three that made up the inner circle of the twelve apostles. The other two were Peter and James. These three were especially privileged to be chosen to be with Jesus at critical times in His life here on earth. For example, they were with Him when He was transfigured (Matthew 17), when He prayed in Gethsemane (Matthew 26) and when He raised Jairus' little daughter from the dead (Mark 5). These same three apostles were prominent also when Jesus instructed His apostles on how to catch fish (Luke 5). What a contrast that is—raise the dead and instruct on fishing.

The apostle John was supernaturally equipped to write the Gospel of John, one of the four Gospels. Each Gospel was written with a unique way of setting forth Jesus. John's book presents Jesus as the Son of God. Matthew's presents Jesus as the King of Israel. Mark's sets forth Jesus as the divine Servant, and Luke's Gospel pictures Jesus as the Son of Man.

When I thought about writing this book on Portraits of Jesus, one of my wife's hobbies came to mind. Pearl takes and collects pictures regularly and seriously. She identifies each one before putting it in an album by writing on the back the name of the persons or scene, the place and date taken. All Pearl's pictures are clearly identified, in other words. When anyone looks at them, no guess work is necessary as to who, when or where, and sometimes even why.

In the Gospel of John the apostle has given us at least 29 portraits of Jesus that unmistakably identify Him as God the Son. Each one is carefully identified and prominently displayed for our instruction and delight. That is what this little book is all about—learning some of the ways Jesus is portrayed in each of the 21 chapters of John's Gospel. It is very important that we remember as we gaze upon these portraits that we are looking at the Lord Jesus Christ, the Son of the Living God.

As I write this book, I view my readers as primarily lay people. My purpose is not to give an exposition of John's Gospel. Rather, it is my wish that when this book is read and responded to, the reader will be assisted in thinking through or walking through John's Gospel with the help of these portraits. I hope I have made it easy to do that for individuals, members of Sunday School classes, or Bible Study classes. Happy looking and learning as you gaze upon John's portraits of Jesus.

Personal applications and study questions are included at the end of each chapter to help the reader be a better person and better acquainted with Jesus, God's beloved Son.

God's Revealer and Revelation

Portrait 1

John 1:1–18

How wonderful it is that the true and living God is not mute. Suppose for a moment that God had not made Himself known, had not revealed Himself at all, ever. That's hard to even imagine, isn't it? How would we know right from wrong? How would we know how to get to heaven or even if there is a heaven or a hell, for that matter? We would not know what God expects of us if He had not revealed Himself. The fact of the matter is we would not even know if God exists or not if He had not spoken. We would not know how we got here either or what the chief end of man is.

But, thankfully, God has made Himself known; He has revealed Himself. He has done this in His Written Word and in His Living Word as well as in His world around us. The Bible, the Written Word of God, claims to be His message to mankind. In God's Written Word He has said that the heavens declare, they tell of, God's glory and their expanse declares His work (Psalm 19:1). To all, God has given evidence of the reality of His existence (Romans. 1:19).

The personal revelation of God was made when Jesus was born of Mary. He is both the personal Revelation of God and He gave God's revelation to mankind as He taught. He made God known to us both by who He was and by what He said. Nobody has ever seen God fully; but Jesus Himself explained God the Father who is Spirit (John 4:4). Jesus laid Him bare, as it were, to the scrutiny of mankind. Only Jesus could do this because He alone is "the only begotten God who is in the bosom of the Father" (1:18). He was sent, was given, by God the Father to the world so that no human need ever perish (3:16).

3

When Jesus was here on earth, He claimed many times to be God's Revelation, God's Messenger. He also while here on planet earth gave many messages, many revelations, about God the Father and how humans can have personal relationships with Him. Jesus revealed God to individuals, small groups, large multitudes, the rich, the poor, the young, the older, the rulers, and the common people.

The first portrait of Jesus we want to see and stand back and admire from John's brush is Jesus as God's Revelation of Himself (vv. 1–18). Jesus as God's Revelation is portrayed in a rather unusual way. He is described as "the Word" who existed before He was born of Mary. His birth had nothing to do with His origin, His beginning. Do you know of any one else of whom this is true? First, then, we might call Him the eternal Word or the Pre-Incarnate Word of God (vv. 1–13) which describes His existence before He was miraculously conceived in Mary's womb. In the same chapter John then presents Jesus as the incarnate Word of God (vv. 14–18). In both cases He is God's Revelation to man.

Let's step up a little closer now and observe some specifics about both of these poses of Jesus as God's Revelation to us.

Jesus, the Eternal, Pre-Incarnate Word of God (vv. 1–13)

How can we be sure the "Word" John writes about here is in fact a reference to Jesus? The answer to this important question is in verse 14 where we read, "And the Word became flesh and dwelt among us."

Jesus of Nazareth, though fully human, is unlike all other humans who ever lived or ever will live. In addition to being fully human He is also fully divine and therefore is the God-Man. It is the divine side, the God side, that John stresses in all his portraits of Jesus.

The "beginning" John wrote about in which Jesus was already present (v. 1) refers to an eternal beginning. This "beginning" is in striking contrast to the "beginning" of Genesis 1:1 which was a point in time when God created the heavens and the earth. The "beginning" in John 1:1 is also in contrast to the "beginning" in 1 John 1:1 which refers to the "beginning" of the Christian era. John makes his point very clear. Jesus as the Word, the Son of God, existed eternally. He was with God. He was God and, of course, still is God.

As God, Jesus created all things. The world was made by Him (vv. 3, 10). Neither unbelieving scientists nor biologists have a verifiable answer to the question, "Where did *life* come from?" The Bible's answer to the question is that life has its source in Jesus. "In Him was life" (v. 4). "Just as the Father has life in Himself, even so He gave to the Son also to have life in Himself" (5:26). Jesus claimed the same for Himself when He said, "I am the way, and the truth, and the life" (14:6).

Jesus, God's personal Revelation, came to His own people, the Jews. He loved them as He loves all mankind. But His own did not accept His love and therefore did not accept Him. They, as a nation, did not receive Him except for a small believing remnant. They rejected God's Revelation to them. What a horrible offense unbelief was and always is.

The rejected personal Revelation of God welcomed all who did receive Him then as He does now. In fact, He exercised His divine power, His authority, and made them "children of God" (v. 12) because they believed in His name.

Jesus, the Incarnate Word of God (vv. 14–18)

Three statements of fact are recorded by John in verse 14. First, "The Word became flesh." Second, this eternal word who became flesh "dwelt among us." Third, the apostle wrote, "we beheld His glory."

The fact that Jesus became flesh makes clear that He did not possess flesh in His pre-incarnate state. No, He was born, He tabernacled among the people He came to redeem. The glory Jesus displayed was not just seen by John the apostle. We know that because John said, "*We* beheld it." This very likely refers to the time when Peter, John, and James, the three on the inner circle of the apostles whom Jesus chose, beheld Jesus on the Mount of Transfiguration (Matthew 17).

We might ask, What was it John and those with him beheld? What did they see? What is meant by "His glory"? The glory of God as used in the Bible refers to the visible manifestation of all that God is. John and his friends were given a glimpse of this as they gazed upon Jesus. The fullness of His grace and truth as God's personal Revealer and Revelation must have nearly blinded them.

John the Baptist gave testimony about Jesus as the very Revelation of God (vv. 14–17). This man was the one who introduced Jesus to the people. He was Jesus' forerunner. He prepared the way for Jesus. He too, along with his friends, witnessed the grace and truth through Jesus Christ. They were given the same revelation of Jesus as was given to John the apostle and those with him.

There are two additional statements of fact in verse18. One, no human has ever seen God in all His fulness. He is Spirit and therefore not visible with the human eye. The real essence of God is invisible. He did appear at times, however, in visible form in Old Testament times, but never in all His fullness. Two, the only begotten God, the Lord Jesus Christ, did explain Him. Jesus, as the Son of God, exposed God to mankind. He did this while here on earth, especially during the three years of His public ministry. Truly, He is the personal Revealer and Revelation of God. Thus, verse 18 is the key that unlocks the door of this portrait of Jesus.

Personal Application

How does this portrait of Jesus as God's personal Revelation of Himself relate to you and me? What differences should this portrait of Jesus make in our lives? There are at least three ways: first, we need to accept and remember the fact that Jesus is God's personal Revelation to us. He is this through what He said and did which is recorded in the New Testament.

Second, God would have us be personal revelations of Him to others. That is His will for all His children. We are told we are His ambassadors. The question is, "How well are we representing Him?"

Third, the only revelation about God that some will ever see or hear will come from us. Those of us who profess to be Christians, God's children, are the only Bible some will ever read. What message are you giving them? We need to think seriously and often about that question.

Study Questions

1. What is the difference between Jesus in His pre-incarnate state and His incarnate state?

2. Can you think of several examples of Jesus giving revelation or messages to the people of His day?

3. How was Jesus as the personal Revelation of God received?

4. How do you suppose you could be God's revelation of Jesus to your children, to your fellow workers, to your friends, and to your neighbors?

5. Are there any ways you can improve as God's personal revelation of Him?

Lamb of God

Portrait 2

John 1:19–51

JOHN THE Baptist was in some ways the Billy Graham of his day. When he preached, even in the wilderness of Judea, throngs of people came from everywhere to hear him. John the Baptist was the forerunner of Jesus the Messiah. In fact, some of those who came thought he was Israel's Messiah. John wasted no time denying this. From his own testimony he was simply the announcer, the herald, of Jesus the Messiah.

This man John the Baptist was truly "sent from God' (John 1:6). He witnessed of Christ in his preaching and his claims. The majority of those who came to hear John were very likely Jews. His call for repentance, a change of mind, was primarily directed to Jews (v. 31). These to whom John ministered needed to change their mind about Jesus, themselves, and their need of Him.

It appears that many of the Jews thought since they were members of the nation which God chose as His own in a unique sense, they were already rightly related to God. They had no need of the repentance John was calling for in his preaching. They were wrong about that. Jehovah God requires an individual response of faith regardless of one's nationality, family, or status in life. This is why John called them all to repentance and faith in Jesus. Faith and repentance are like two sides of the same coin. One cannot have faith without repentance or a change of mind about one's self and the Savior. But it would be possible to have a genuine change of mind without faith or acceptance of Christ as Savior. It is very likely that many come to realize they need to change their ways and do so, but never do trust Jesus as their Substitute for sin.

John the Baptist's Witness of Jesus as the Lamb of God, vv. 19–34

John the baptizer set forth a twofold witness of Jesus as the Lamb of God. The first witness was his baptizing of repentant Jews in water. Their identification, which is what baptism means, demonstrated before others their acknowledgment that Jesus was Israel's Messiah and their Savior. The water was and always is without any saving merit. Rather, being baptized by John meant that they truly had repented, changed their minds about Jesus, and embraced Him as their own personal Savior.

It appears that before John baptized anyone, he needed to respond to the questions thrown at him. Priests and Levites from Jerusalem sent by the Pharisees asked him who he was. John must have known that some among the Jews thought he was the Messiah. He assured them that he was not the Christ, the Messiah, promised in their Old Testament. "Are you Elijah then," they asked, and he answered, "No, I am not." "Are you any one of the other great prophets?" they asked. Again he answered, "No, I am not."

John then told those who were sent to ask Him these questions that he was only like the voice of one crying in the wilderness calling for the nation to make ready for and accept Jesus the Messiah. His questioners appear perplexed at John's answers. They asked him another question, "Why are you baptizing Jews in the Jordan?" His response to this question gave John occasion to do what God had called him to do—to introduce them to Jesus. Here then we have the beautiful portrait of Jesus as the Lamb of God, His sacrifice for sin.

This Lamb is God's Lamb. Unlike any of the lambs sacrificed by the Jews before, Jesus *"takes away* the sin of the *world"* (v. 29). This is the key verse for this portrait of Jesus. Among the Jews there had to be repeated sacrifices of lambs year after year continually. Why was this necessary? It was because the sacrifice of those lambs merely covered sin for the period between the sacrifices. In striking contrast, the one sacrifice of Jesus, God's Lamb, on the cross took away the sin. It was a full, final, forever sacrifice, not just for the sin of some but for the sin of the whole world of mankind. However, just as in the old economy's sacrificial system where the one making the sacrifice needed to believe God—that the sacrifice covered the sin until the next time of sacrifice—so the sacrifice, the substitution Jesus made, must be received by faith in order to be beneficial (v. 12).

The second witness John the Baptist gave of Jesus as the Lamb of God was of Jesus' baptism with the Holy Spirit. This baptism was still future

8

when John wrote. He contrasted his baptism of Jews who had repented with that of Jesus' baptism "in the Holy Spirit" (v. 33). Jesus was the all-important One, not John. What John the Baptist did was prepare the way, remind the Jews that their Messiah had come and would identify them with the Holy Spirit, the Third Member of the Godhead.

John tells us in another portrait he paints of Jesus that Jesus would send the Holy Spirit after His return to the Father (John 16:7). The apostle Paul made clear that when the Holy Spirit would come, He would baptize believing sinners into the body of Christ (1 Corinthians 12:12–13). So, who then would be the Agent in this Spirit baptism, Jesus or the Spirit Himself? The answer is that both the Spirit and Jesus are Agents in Spirit baptism. Jesus is the Agent because He sent the Holy Spirit. So is the Spirit the Agent because of Paul's clear statement in 1 Corinthians 12:12. This baptism in the Spirit and by the Spirit began on the Day of Pentecost (Acts 2).

This portrait of Jesus as the Lamb of God included Him as the Son of God (John 1:34).

Jesus' Disciples' Witness of Jesus as the Lamb of God, vv. 35–51

Andrew and Simon apparently followed after Jesus in response to John the Baptist's calling Him "the Lamb of God" (vv. 36–37). When Jesus saw them following Him, He asked them what they wanted. Their answer was, "Where are You staying?" Jesus then invited them to come with Him. They stayed until about "the tenth hour" (v. 39) which was 10:00 a.m. Roman time and 4:00 p.m. Jewish time.

Andrew and Simon Peter were brothers and the former introduced the latter to Jesus. What a beautiful picture we have here of how without any formal Biblical training, Andrew introduced his brother Peter to Jesus. As far as we know, Andrew was not a great preacher, not very famous. However, one thing he knew for sure, he had found the long-awaited Messiah. And from that day on in every reference of him in Scripture he is bringing someone to Jesus (John 1:42; 6:8–9; 12:20–22)

Philip and Nathanael also were a part of this portrait of Jesus as the Lamb of God. In the case of Philip, Jesus sought him out. Would he have come to Jesus on his own later? We do not know for sure but very likely he would have come. When Jesus found Philip, He said to him, "Follow Me" (v. 43). This man was from the same city as Andrew and Peter were. That was the city of Bethsaida, north and east of Nazareth in Galilee.

After Philip met Jesus, he wasted no time to introduce Him to his friend Nathanael. We have found the Messiah promised in our Scripture he told Nathanael. He is the One whom Moses wrote about. He was fully convinced that Jesus met all the requirements predicted of the Messiah.

At first Nathanael was not so sure that Philip was right about his claim. The city of Nazareth had a bad reputation in those days. Many questioned whether any good thing could come out of it. Philip knew all about what many thought of Nazareth; but to convince his friend that Jesus was a unique exception to the damaging slogan, he said, "Come and see" (v. 46).

When Jesus, the Lamb of God, saw Nathanael coming toward Him, He commended him for being an Israelite without deceit or guile (v. 47). This shocked Nathanael, and he bravely asked Jesus how He knew him. Remember, as far as we know, Nathanael had not met Jesus before this encounter. Jesus obliged him with His answer. "I saw you one day when you were under a fig tree before Philip ever called you to come and meet me." That commendation from Jesus and the fact that He had seen Nathanael under the fig tree convinced Nathanael that Jesus was all He claimed to be, very God of very God. Most certainly the Spirit of God had prepared him for this encounter with Jesus. Because he had believed the minimal revelation about Jesus, God would grant him greater and fuller revelation.

Personal Application

You may be asking, So what? Jesus is the Lamb of God whom John portrayed in the passage studied here. How does that relate to me or affect me? First, this portrait should remind us that we all need a sacrifice for our sin that satisfies God. Adam and Eve tried to make themselves acceptable to God by covering themselves with fig leaves. That did not satisfy God. He rejected their efforts and made them a covering from an animal caught in a thicket. And remember, God requires a perfect sacrifice and only He could provide that. Second, if we have accepted God's Lamb as our Savior, our Sacrifice, we should be sharing Him with others just like Andrew and Philip did.

Study Questions

1. Name some unique things about John the Baptist.

2. Why did the Jews think they did not need John's message?

3.   What exactly was the heart of John's message?

4.   When did the baptism by the Spirit occur?

5.   What examples did Andrew and Philip set for us?

The One with Divine Authority

Portrait 3

John 2

Genuine credentials are always necessary to establish one's authority over others. Such authority may be verified in a number of ways. A policeman's uniform, his badge, and his revolver by his side silently announce his authority. When the president of the United States chooses and sends an ambassador to another country, that person must have the credentials to verify his role as ambassador. From that point on he or she is then acknowledged as an official representative of the USA.

Jesus' Authority at a Wedding, vv. 1–11

As Jesus began His public ministry as the Son of God on earth, He early on gave convincing evidence that He was who He claimed to be and whom He had come to make known. In John 2 we see that Jesus chose to demonstrate His authority to two different groups of people at two different occasions and locations. The first was at a wedding. This first group was for the most part His friends. At least those present at the great social event were not trying to find fault with Him.

The wedding incident took place soon after Jesus had been introduced to the people by John the Baptist as the Lamb of God. It could very well be that Mary, Jesus' mother, was related to the family of the bride or, at the very least, well acquainted with them. Such a connection could have been the reason Jesus and His disciples were invited. That was a great honor, to be sure. As the events unfold, it becomes very obvious that Mary had accepted Jesus' authority. Had the disciples done so? Had the other guests at the wedding done so?

Interestingly, among the people in that part of the world there were three stages to observe in a wedding. The first stage was the legal stage in which the parents of the bride and the bridegroom agreed on the wedding.

Second, the bridegroom would come to claim his bride, to take her to his home prepared for her. Third, there was a wedding feast where there was happy celebration. It appears that the wedding Jesus and His disciples attended was the third stage with all the festivities.

The problem that arose at this wedding was an embarrassing one indeed. Put yourself in the shoes of the host and hostess of this family. Imagine at your daughter's or son's wedding there were not enough refreshments—wedding cake or drinks—to go around. What a social blunder and embarrassment that would be. In the Middle East culture it would have been a social error that was almost unforgivable. But that is precisely what happened at this wedding. They ran out of wine (v. 3).

There was the risk that if there was not enough wine, the newly married couple would be disgraced and maybe even avoided by the people among whom they would live. In that culture in that country at this time, this was a huge problem.

Little wonder then that Mary took it upon herself to go to Jesus with the problem. We cannot help but wonder how Mary knew the wine was all gone. This may be good reason to believe Jesus' mother knew the family very well and maybe even assisted in serving the guests. The fact that she knew about the problem and sought to relieve the parents of consequences that would follow and came to Jesus for help indicates she was a special guest who knew the family and, more importantly, knew Jesus.

Mary's coming to Jesus reveals she knew He could do something about the situation. Surely she was aware of John's baptism of Jesus and the divine approval of Jesus given there. The disciples of her Son had been called and responded to follow Jesus. Mary must have known that too. Her appeal to Jesus gives evidence that she had accepted His divine authority. She believed in Him.

At first glance Jesus' response to Mary appears to be a bit rude. He said to her, "Woman, what do I have to do with you? My hour has not yet come" (v. 4). In our culture one's mother is not usually addressed in that way. But in the Middle East culture of that day Jesus' words were not viewed as disrespectful. To the contrary, "woman" was a term of respect and affection. Jesus used the same term of His mother when He was on the cross (19:26) where He was showing love and care for her.

The response to Mary's implied request demonstrates Jesus' authority. No longer was He under her authority, and Joseph His adopted father is believed to have died earlier (v. 4a). Jesus had entered His public ministry at about the age of 30. He was acting on His own diviine authority now and gently reminded Mary of that and that His "hour had not yet come"

(v. 4b) meaning the hour for which He came into the world, His death on the cross.

The key verse for this portrait of Jesus sums up His awesome divine authority. "His mother said to the servants, "Whatever He says to you, do it." (v. 5). Mary obviously had complete trust in Jesus' authority and ability to remedy the situation. She may not have known just what He would do; but she knew He could fix the problem. Her Son was not only a man but was at the same time also God. How awesome!

Close by, were 6 large stone waterpots or jars. These were used usually for the Jewish custom of purification and so held washing water (v. 6). They each held between 20 or 30 gallons of water according to our measurements. The Law of Moses and some traditions under which the people lived required various cleansings. Most likely the reference to "Jews" here refers to the Jewish leaders.

The command of Jesus was clear enough: "Fill the waterpots with water" (v. 7). But the question of why this was to be done surely must have puzzled them. In response to what Mary told them, they followed the orders. Since Jesus told them to do it, they must have respected Him and His right to make the demand.

No sooner than they filled the jars, Jesus must have surprised them with another command. Give some to the "headwaiter," He told them (v. 8). And they again did as they were told but were probably a bit hesitant. The "headwaiter" was the one in charge of the banquet who tasted the food and drink before they were served to the invited guests. After he tasted the miracle-wine, he called for the bridegroom. "You have kept the best until last," the headwaiter told him. This was a compliment since often the poorest wine was kept back for serving last (v. 10). There is no reason to read into the words of the headwaiter that he meant the guests were nearly drunk at that time. Jesus certainly would not have sanctioned drunkenness by providing wine for the guests. His miracle-wine would not have made them drunk in the first place.

Imagine it, what normally took much work and a long period of time, Jesus accomplished instantly by His creative power. Much time and effort have been spent in argumentation whether the wine Jesus produced was fermented or not. There are two kinds of wines referred to in the Bible. One was alcoholic and the other nonalcoholic which was made from fruit juices. I believe we can be sure Jesus did not create an intoxicating wine. I like to refer to the wine Jesus made as miracle-wine.

As far as the disciples with Him were concerned, Jesus "manifested His glory," or His divine Sonship. He demonstrated His authority and they believed in Him (v. 11).

Jesus' Authority in the Temple, vv. 12–25

From Cana where Jesus demonstrated His authority by turning water into wine, He, His mother, brothers and disciples went to Capernaum on the northwest side of the Sea of Galilee. They spent a few days there and then He and the disciples went to Jerusalem for the Passover observance. This was one of the national feasts of the Jews. It was in memory of their miraculous deliverance from Egypt and Pharaoh's cruel hand.

There in the temple Jesus found what had become a sacrilegious use of the outer court of the temple. This area had been set aside for the convenience of the many who came from far away. They normally did not bring their animals along for sacrifice, and they had to purchase the animals there. Also, they brought foreign currency and needed to exchange it for the Jewish shekels since foreign currency could not be used in the temple.

Over a period of time, those who sold the animals for sacrifice and those who exchanged money found what they were doing to be very lucrative business. What started out to be a necessary service in the temple court had become a loud, boisterous, bargaining, competitive, money-making racket.

When Jesus, therefore, drove the money-changers and merchants out and overthrew their tables, He did so because His "Father's house had been made a house of merchandise" (v. 16). Jesus was not opposed to the original intent in providing for those who came from distant lands. What He was opposed to was the greed and materialism with which the business was conducted. Such behavior was totally inconsistent with the purpose for which the Passover was established.

Three responses resulted from Jesus' display of His authority in the temple. The first was from the Jewish leaders. What right, by what authority, do you do this, they asked Him. Remember these were His critics who demanded an explanation. They wanted a sign, a miracle, to prove to them that Jesus was who He claimed to be, God the Father's Son, the Messiah. He did say the temple was His Father's house as He chased the merchants out (v. 16).

The answer Jesus gave to the Jews was not understood by them. He said, "you want a sign, here is the sign I'll give you to prove my authority.

"Destroy this temple, and in three days I will raise it up" (v. 19). He was referring to His own death at their hands and His bodily resurrection at God's hand. All they could think of was how long it had taken to build their temple—"forty-six years," they said (v. 20).

The second response was from the disciples. They did not seem to understand at the time what Jesus meant either. But when Jesus was actually bodily raised from the dead and they not only looked into the empty tomb, but they also walked, talked, and even ate with Him in His resurrection body, then they understood. This post-resurrection experience reminded them what Jesus had said when asked for a sign of His authority.

There was a third response to the demonstration of Jesus' authority in the temple. It came from some of the people who had witnessed Jesus' miraculous power displayed before their very eyes. Most likely, not everyone who claimed to believe in Him did so sincerely and for the right reason. Jesus knew then, and He has known ever since to this very hour, who has genuinely trusted Him and who has not.

Personal Application

What lessons can we learn from this portrait of Jesus as the One with divine authority? How can we apply these things to ourselves? Here are a couple of suggestions: (1) Jesus alone has the authority, the power, to save sinners and who of us is not one? He does not force anyone to accept Him as their Substitute for sin. He and His saving authority must be received by faith and (2) Jesus also wants to be on the throne of our lives. He wants authority over us. That means we need to surrender to His control. Someone is on the throne of everyone's life. Either we are or God is. Jesus longs to be not only our Savior but also our Lord.

Study Questions

1. How did Jesus show His divine authority at the wedding?

2. What role did Mary His mother have in His demonstration of authority?

3. Why do you think Jesus was so willing to demonstrate His authority so early in His public ministry?

4. What exactly was the problem in the temple experience?

5. There were three responses to what Jesus did in the temple. What were they?

6. What are some ways you can allow Jesus to be more in control of your life?

Savior of Sinners

Portrait 4

John 3

NOT ALL of Jesus' people, called "His own" (John 1:11), rejected Him out of hand. Some did sincerely want to know more about Him; some did believe "in His name" (2:23). Nicodemus was very likely one of these even though he was "a ruler of the Jews" (3:1). How to know God for sure and have eternal life must have been why he came to Jesus. As the Son of God, Jesus read Nicodemus' mind, as it were, and gave him the answer to his question even before he asked it. Jesus made it abundantly clear that He alone was the Savior of sinners and apart from Him there was no salvation. Jesus told him right up front that he needed to be born again.

Jesus and Nicodemus, vv. 1–21

The two met personally for the first time, it seems, when Nicodemus came to Jesus. Rabbi teacher, he called Him. This was a term of respect. God must be with you, you must come from Him, Nicodemus insisted, because of the signs or miracles you are performing. This "ruler" was different than most of the others in that he did not reject Jesus out of hand.

Nicodemus was not just an average Jew either. He mwas a member of the Sanhedrin, one of the highest classes in Judaism, consisting of 70 or 72 teachers, rulers, of the nation. Added to this honor, this man was also a Pharisee. That tells us he was a devoted believer in the Old Testament and a strict interpreter of its laws. As a group, the Pharisees were well-intentioned but spiritually blind to who Jesus really was. We do not know for sure why Nicodemus came to Jesus by night. Maybe it was because he was fearful of being seen by his peers. More likely, it was because he wanted to visit with Jesus alone and that would be easier to do at night.

The response Jesus gave Nicodemus seems a bit abrupt at first sight. He ignored completely the high commendations which Nicodemus gave

Him. Instead, Jesus went immediately to the real issue. The interested ruler had a much greater need than an answer as to how Jesus did what He did. Nicodemus needed to be born again first; then his surface and general questions could be answered. In essence, what Jesus said to him was, Here is how you and anyone else can get into the kingdom of God, can get rightly related to God, and have eternal life.

How does one become born again? That is what the puzzled ruler of the Jews then asked Jesus. He was confused and expressed his confusion very clearly. Nicodemus knew no one could ever be physically reborn. And even if that were possible, how would that equip one to see the kingdom of God? This ruler knew he needed a new start in life. Being a ruler of the Jews apparently did not give Him any assurance of eternal life with God. That is sad, is it not? This man was not a wicked person. Why did he and his peers need such a transformation which only a new birth could provide? And how could he get it if he wanted it?

Entrance into the kingdom of God, Jesus said, required two births—one physical and the other spiritual. "Unless one is born of water and the Spirit, he cannot enter into the kingdom of God" (v. 5). The water Jesus referred to was the water sack housing the fetus in the womb. Before physical birth this must be broken. This seems to be the meaning of the "water" Jesus spoke of to Nicodemus. Contextually, it fits perfectly with the questions he raised. In this way, the inadequacy of physical birth alone was stressed. Jesus spoke similarly as He comforted Martha when she mourned her brother Lazurus' death. On that occasion He said, ". . . everyone who lives and believes in me will never die" (Luke 11:26). Of course, one must live before he or she can believe in Jesus. Here again, Jesus was teaching that physical life does not equip one for heaven.

Do not try to understand what I have said to you, Jesus told Nicodemus. Then he illustrated from nature how even though we know the wind blows, yet we do not know where it comes from or where it's going. So it is with the Spirit-produced new birth (v. 8). It is all of God and must be experienced by faith.

Nicodemus' question, "How can these things be?" (v. 9) shows his genuine interest in what Jesus was saying. He was groping for an answer. Jesus gently reminded him that as a religious teacher of the Jews, he should have known what was being told him (v. 10). Jesus and His disciples spoke the truth but their testimony was not believed by many including Nicodemus (v. 11). Further, Jesus said to him that he had not believed what He had told him about earthly things and the liklihood was that neither would he believe what He said about heavenly things (v. 12).

It is difficult to know for sure whether verses 16 to 21 continues Jesus' conversation with Nicodemus or represents John's own words as he summarizes Jesus' teaching regardingt the new birth. Evangelical scholarship is divided over this issue. It seems to me that these verses constitute the words of John the apostle as he was led by the Spirit to write.

The key verse in John's summary and in the entire chapter is verse 16. Without doubt, it is the most often quoted verse in the entire Bible. It states clearly the extent and degree of God's love, the greatest gift ever given, the condition of salvation and the promise of eternal life to those who believe.

Why will many never experience the eternal life which Jesus referred to? Could it be they just did not work hard enough, did not do enough good works? Or could it be the fact that they were born in sin and committed terrible sins? No, regardless whether Jesus said it or John, it is precisely recorded that it is because they have "not believed in the name of the only begotten Son of God" (vv. 17–18) that they will experience eternal condemnation. Of course, it is true that because of their sin, they commit the greatest sin of all—reject Jesus the gift of God's love.

Jesus and John the Baptist, vv. 22–36

The second part of this chapter (chap. 3) is introduced by "after these things." John uses this phrase several times in his Gospel (cf. 3:22; 2:12; 5:1; 6:1 and 7:1). The meaning is not that what follows took place immediately after what preceded. John selected, and was guided by the Spirit to select those things in Jesus' life on earth which were in keeping with his purpose. That purpose is clearly stated as "that you may believe that Jsus is the Christ, the Son of God; and that believing you may have life in His name (20:30–31).

While Jesus and His disciples stayed on for a while in Judaea and baptized repentant Jews, John the Baptist was ministering near Salem (vv. 22–23). This was very likely a Samaritan town near the Jordan River. Jews there were responding to John's message about Jesus and were being baptized by him. Some time later, perhaps soon after this, he was thrown into prison (v. 24).

John the Baptist was a truly humble man, a humble servant of the Lord. He fulfilled his calling by announcing Jesus the Messiah's coming and by preparing for His coming. After his work was finished, he stepped back so attention would be on Jesus, not on himself. John was blessed to have witnessed the Holy Spirit represented by a dove descend on Jesus at

His baptism. He also heard the voice of God the Father say, "Thou art My beloved Son, in Thee I am well-pleased" (Mark 1:11).

It appears that some of John's disciples disputed over some "purification" issue (3:25). This was no doubt the same custom referred to at the wedding in Cana (2:6). The dispute may even have been over John evangelizing and baptizing Samaritans who were treated like dogs by many Jews at that time.

Some Jews came to John calling him "Rabbi" with a question (v. 26). It centered over the fact that Jesus was getting more attention and having more converts than the John the Baptist was having. The language used here suggests there was some bitterness in the hearts of these people. Perhaps they feared they were losing some popularity and hold on the people because John the Baptist's disciples were many and they were following Jesus.

Without any hesitation, John responded to these disciples of his with much the same as he had given them before. His answer to their perceived problem was, "He must increase, but I must decrease" (v. 30).

It seems that John the apostle gives a summary with further explanation in verses 31 to 36 of what John the Baptist said about Jesus. In other words, John the Baptist's words appear to conclude with verse 30. What follows in verses 31 to 36 seems to be the words of John the apostle. In these verses he gives profound statements about Jesus the Savior of sinners. Jesus is "From above" (v. 31). His origin is eternal (vv. 31–35). He did not begin to exist in Bethlehem's barn and manger. Jesus bears witness of God. He gave a divine testimony. Everything that Jesus says is from God. Those who receive what He says are at the same time accepting what God says. They are hearing from heaven! Jesus has received His authority from God. He has the Holy Spirit. He is filled or controlled by the Spirit.

This chapter which gives us the portrait of Jesus as the Savior of sinners concludes with the same emphasis given earlier in verses 16 to 18. In both passages those who believe, who receive Jesus as their Substitute for sin, are given eternal life. Those who do not receive Him will perish" (v. 16) and will experience "the wrath of God" (v. 36). The "eternal life" God gives to believing sinners does not begin at death. It commences the instant the new birth takes place. Those who will experience "the wrath of God" (v. 36) or eternal condemnation will do so because they have not accepted God's love in Christ.

Personal Application

Personal applications from this portrait of Jesus include our need to be forgiven by God, to be born again. Regardless how good or religious we may be, we need to be born from above just as Nicodemus did. He was a good religious man too. Surely, no one wants to experience God's wrath. Yet that is what will happen to all who do not accept Jesus the Savior of sinners as their own Savior.

Jesus did not tell Nicodemus to add more good works to things he was already doing. The only way he or anyone else can avoid eternal condemnation is to be born again, born from above.

Study Questions

1. What do you think attracted Nicodemus to Jesus the Savior of sinners?

2. Do you have any idea why Nicodemus chose to come to Jesus at night?

3. How was Jesus able to know what was on Nicodemus' mind before he even asked?

4. What is the key verse in this chapter? Can you quote it?

5. Can you think of ways you can present the gospel message of this chapter to someone today or tomorrow?

Meeting People's Needs

Portrait 5

John 4

CARING, CONCERN, and compassion for others is in short supply these days sometimes even among Christians. When it comes right down to it, many of us are a pretty selfish and self-centered lot. And to behave that way is really an animalistic trait.

Have you ever seen any hungry animal share its food with other animals at the trough? I have not but then maybe there are some rare exceptions. I know animals often eat out of the same dish or trough but I mean do they ever leave any intentionally for others? I do not think so. Do they ever find food and enlist others to share it with them? No!

Recently there have been some happy and welcome exceptions to our normally selfish and self-centered living. For instance, when the 9/11 terrorist attack in 2001 against the United States occurred, there was a widespread response of help regardless of race, color, or creed. After the Tsunami disaster in 2004 many countries gave millions of dollars for relief efforts. More recently, the Katrina hurricane tragedy in New Orleans and neighboring states in August, 2005 brought rescue efforts of all kinds from all across the United States to help the trapped and needy.

Throughout His life on earth Jesus was constantly seeking out people with needs and then meeting those needs for them. This portrait of Jesus is especially prominent in John 4. Here we see how He met the needs of a sinner, some saints, and a seeker.

But before we meet these people and watch Jesus and see how He met their needs, let's observe where He and John the Baptist were and how He came upon the first needy soul. In the first four verses of John 4 we are told how Jesus became quite popular after John the Baptist introduced Him as the Lamb of God. People who had been following John left him and began following Jesus (v. 1). His disciples were baptizing more people who had believed than John the Baptist baptized. Jesus and His disciples left Judea and headed north to Galilee (v. 3). When traveling between Galilee and Jerusalem Jews usually avoided going through Samaria. Why? Because the people who lived there, the Samaritans, were usually hated and despised because they were not full-blooded Jews.

Jesus, however, "had to pass through Samaria" (v. 4) enroute to Galilee. He "had to"? Samaria was avoided like the plague by going the long way around it. Why then did Jesus "need" to go through Samaria? Was it because He was in a hurry? Was He fleeing from someone? No, it was because He had an important message for the people of the city. They needed to know of God's love for them. Jesus did not come to earth to minister only to Jews. He came to seek and save the lost—all of them—regardless of color, race, gender, or creed. Later in the story Jesus reminded His disciples that His food was "to do the will of Him who sent Me and to accomplish His work" (v. 34). This is the key verse for this portrait of Jesus.

A Woman of the World, vv. 5–26

While enroute to Samaria, Jesus came to Sychar, a city in Samaria. This small town was close by some land that years before Jacob gave to his son Joseph. Even more important than that, there was a water well there that Jacob had dug. This well was the divinely appointed place for Jesus and His disciples to stop and rest and be refreshed after a long and tiring day of travel.

Jesus was sitting beside the well resting at about 12:00 noon according to Jewish time. This would have been 6:00 p.m. by Roman time. From what follows in the story, Jesus did not have any way of getting water from the well as it was customarily done. He was so divine that He knew the woman of Samaria's need yet He was so human that He was tired and thirsty and wanted help to get the water from the well.

We do not know how long He was there before the woman came to get water for her own use. We do know the disciples had been sent into the nearby City of Sychar to buy food, which means Jesus was there alone when the woman came. He said to her, "Give Me a drink" (v. 7). He spoke first and asked a favor of the woman, a Samaritan woman. That was most unusual.

Of course, Jesus was not surprised when the woman came. He, as the Son of God, not only knew she would come. He knew also precisely when she would come. And He knew who she was, a woman of the street who was living an immoral life. It was not therefore an accident or a mere coincidence that Jesus was there and she came there at the same time. This woman had a great need in her life, and Jesus began to meet her need immediately.

A rather lively question and answer session followed Jesus' request of the woman. She responded in shock and amazement. She said, "How is it that you, being a Jew, ask me for a drink, since I am a Samaritan woman?" (v. 9). The woman and Jesus both knew full well that Jews, for the most part, just had no dealings with the Samaritans. It was understandable for her to raise the issue. After all, what Jesus was doing was most unusual. Two things concerned her deeply. First, she was a Samaritan and He was a Jew. Second, she was a woman and was there alone with the man Jesus and that was not at all normative in that culture.

Jesus' reply to her related to her need for "living water" (v. 10)—salvation. She needed the gift God would give her for the taking. At this point she, of course, did not know that Jesus the Son of God, the Messiah, was the One who asked her for a drink. It is important to note that Jesus did not scold the woman for her sinful lifestyle but instead presented to her the gift of salvation. Changes in her life were needed but would come after she had received the gift, and they would not hinder her from receiving the gift.

Jesus alone was the One who could give the quality of water which would quench her thirst forever (vv. 10, 14). But how and where could He get this water? The woman must have been thinking of some special kind of physical water. Jesus did not have any means of getting it there. Since He was a Jew and she was a Samaritan, He could not use the bucket and rope she brought with her because the "Jews had no dealings with the Samaritans" (v. 9).

Great as he was, Jacob, who dug the well and who along with his sons and all his cattle drank from it, was far greater than Jesus as far as she was concerned (v. 12). When Jesus, unlike Jacob, said He could and would give her drink that would keep her from ever thirsting again, the woman asked for it. "Give me this water" (v. 15), she said, so I will not need to come here again.

So that she would understand her deepest need, Jesus told her to go and bring her husband. He knew this woman's heart perfectly. She needed to understand her sin and deep, deep need if she was to receive the gift of God which Jesus offered her. The desire for what Jesus offered her was so great that she did not want to forfeit getting it, so boldly she said, "I have no husband" (v. 17). She in fact did have a man with whom she was living, but he was not her husband.

After Jesus told her He knew of her background, she was shocked and from then on viewed Him as a prophet. She then proceeded to talk about the contrast between Jewish and Samaritan worship (vv. 20–26). Where was the proper place? she wondered. Was it Jerusalem as the Jews believed or was it Mount Gerizim as the Samaritans said? Where one worships, Jesus told her, is not the important thing but one's relationship with God and attitude toward Him is important. In fact, the Father seeks all those who worship Him in spirit and in truth wherever they live.

This woman with all her need did believe Messiah would come. Her statement about this seems to make clear that she believed when Messiah came, He would declare the truth. Then it was that Jesus revealed Himself to her: "I who speak to you am He" (v. 26). Because she was ready to receive the Messiah, Jesus was quick to reveal His identity. To many members of His own nation Jesus did not at first freely make known His Messiahship. The reason for that hesitancy was because of their unbelief.

The story does not end there. The disciples returned from their trip to the city to buy food. Jesus met their need after the woman left to tell her men friends about Jesus.

Willing Workers, vv. 27–42

Just as this woman of the world heard from Jesus that He was the long-promised Messiah and apparently received Him as such, the disciples returned from the trek to the city. She then left her waterpot and went home to tell the men about Jesus (v. 28).

When the disciples first got back to the well where they had left Jesus, they were shocked and amazed. He had been talking to a woman, and a Samaritan at that. They said nothing to Him about their surprise. Instead, they begged Jesus to eat what they had brought. It seems they were quick to begin eating but Jesus was not joining them. His response to their appeal to Him to eat brought even more amazement. His answer to them was that He had food to eat that they did not know anything about (v. 32).

Upon hearing what Jesus said, the disciples discussed among themselves His meaning. Why was He not hungry, they wondered. "Nobody brought Him food, did they?" the disciples asked each other. Knowing their real need was much greater than to find out why He was not hungry, Jesus quickly told them what they truly needed to hear and learn and should never forget.

What they needed so desperately to know was that the reason He had called them to be His followers in the first place was to herald the good news of God's saving grace to all people. They were to work with Him spreading the news and reaping the harvest as well. Some of the harvest was before their very eyes and they did not see it. Look on the fields, He urged them (v. 35). They are ready for harvest. The disciples apparently were so anxious to get to Galilee where there were no Samaritans that they were blind to the needs of the Samaritans all around them. There was fruit there to be gathered for life eternal, and they did not see it.

The disciples must have been totally surprised when the woman of Samaria's men came back with her to the well to meet Jesus. It seems these friends of hers were enamored with Jesus. To begin, they knew Jesus did not look down on them because of their race. At least these men "believed in Him," and they did so because of the testimony of the woman. There were at least five men, it seems (v. 18).

Jesus accepted their invitation to come to the city and stay with them. They wanted to hear more. The disciples must have gone with Him. Imagine what they said to each other and how they reacted when they all stayed two days. More mind boggling still, there was more harvest. "Many more believed because of His word" (v. 41). They assured the woman that it was not just because of her appraisal of Jesus. They had heard Him for themselves and had no doubt that He was "the Savior of the world" (v. 42).

A Worried Official, vv. 43–54

After His two-day visit in Sychar of Samaria, Jesus returned with His disciples to Galilee. The folks there received Him gladly. We might ask why they did this. It was because they had been to the Passover Feast in Jerusalem and witnessed what Jesus did there when He demonstrated His divine authority in the temple (v. 45). Whether their faith was genuine or not it is hard to discern.

It is interesting to note how two different people approached Jesus. The woman of Samaria was not expecting to meet Jesus at the well. The worried official we will meet shortly sought out Jesus because he had a desperate need. Jesus asked a favor of the woman because He was thirsty. The nobleman, or worried official, asked Jesus to come and heal his son. Both the Samaritan woman and the nobleman were called upon by Jesus to believe Him, to exercise faith in Him.

What was it that brought the nobleman to Jesus? Very likely, He knew that Jesus had turned water into wine at Cana. Also, his son was at the point of death in Capernaum (v. 46). So this minor official of Herod's court braved whatever might happen to him and he sought out Jesus for help (v. 47).

The nobleman did not flaunt his status in the Roman court. Rather, he implored Jesus to come with him to Capernaum and heal his son. Jesus' first response to his request was to chide him a bit for being like many others wanting a sign, a miracle before believing in Jesus (v. 48). His remark was not only about the man before Him. He intended His response for any who received Him just because He was a miracle-worker.

This worried official did not try to persuade Jesus that He was sincere in his faith and was an exception. Instead, he said, "Sir, come down before my child dies" (v. 49). With that said, Jesus told him to go back home because his son was not going to die (v. 50). Without any further pleading, the nobleman started off for his home in Capernaum. Capernaum was about 25 miles from Cana which meant it was a long and hard journey.

Enroute, the nobleman was met by some of his servants. They told him that his son is living, he is no longer sick; his fever left him "yesterday at the seventh hour" (v. 52), they said. That did it. No longer was the worried official worried because he knew it was at that very same time Jesus had told him, "Your son lives" (v. 53). Jesus had performed a miracle. He met the worried official's need without ever seeing or touching the lad. Furthermore, the harvest which Jesus referred to with His disciples extended to the nobleman's family and very likely included his servants. His "whole house" believed (v. 53).

This was the second of the eight miracles which Jesus performed in John's record.

Personal Applications

Jesus is still able and willing to meet people's needs. The woman of Samaria did not come to Jesus for help, but she soon learned that she really did need help. Neither did the disciples realize they needed help, but it did not take long until they understood their role in the harvest Jesus was talking about. On the other hand, the nobleman knew he had a need. His son was dying. With Jesus' healing of his son the nobleman came to know and believe Jesus was the answer to his spiritual needs also.

All of us have needs many of which we cannot meet or solve ourselves. We all need Jesus. We need Him first for salvation; we need Him as our Savior. He is the only One who can meet this need. We must never be ashamed or afraid to come to Jesus by faith with our needs. The temptation for many is to view the Lord as a sort of sugar-daddy, eager to give us everything we want. No, there is no promise that God will supply all our wants, but He does promise to supply all our needs (Philippians 4:19).

Study Questions

1. Can you think of lessons you can learn from Jesus' dealing with the woman of Samaria?

2. How does the Jews' treatment of the Samaritans at that time relate to racial prejudices today?

3. Was it wrong for the disciples to go for food and then to worry because Jesus did not want to eat?

4. What lesson did Jesus teach His disciples on this occasion?

5. What resulted from Jesus' work with the worried official?

6. Are you planning to change your behavior this week because of this study? How?

Pursued by Killers

Portrait 6

John 5:1–18

WHILE LOOKING at this portrait of the Lord Jesus, we see Him beside the pool of Bethesda. He is talking to a crippled man who had never walked. Jesus tells him to get up and walk. Can you imagine Jesus saying that to a man who could not walk?

In the background of this picture stands a group of Jews who voiced great opposition to what Jesus did for the cripple. Why? Because at Jesus' command the man picked up his make-shift "bed" and walked. I wonder why that upset the Jews. Why were they not happy that the man, who they knew could not walk previously, could now walk without any help? Did they have no concern for the less fortunate? Apparently not. As we look closer, we will find out why they acted as they did. More than that, we will also discover why these same Jews set out to kill Jesus. These were some He came to save, but they received Him not.

The Miracle That Caused the Pursuit, vv. 1–9

Jesus and His disciples came back to Jerusalem from Galilee for another one of Israel's special feasts, most likely the Passover. As soon as they arrived, they were met with increased rejection and outright hostility from the Jews. While there in that environment, Jesus performed His third miracle recorded by John.

This portrait seems to have been painted right after Jesus had ministered to the woman from Samaria and the nobleman from Cana. There was fierce opposition and rejection of Jesus by members of His own nation. They were determined not to receive Him. Instead, they leveled the most serious charges against Him and even tried to use the Law of Moses as their authority.

The pool of Bethesda was near the sheep gate of the temple. There were five porticoes or cloisters close by the gate apparently to provide shelter for the sick who often gathered there. The St. Anne's church is located close by this gate today. It was here that those with physical infirmities came in search of deliverance.

The pool referred to was longer than it was wide and was used to clean animals that were brought to the temple for sacrifice. The water was not deep and not very clean either. Interestingly, archaeologists have found the remains of such a pool. Bethesda means "house of mercy."

It seems a view developed that there was some healing power in the water which was caused by an angel who visited the pool and stirred up the water (v. 4). The paralyzed man Jesus spoke to there must have believed this, as did others. But he was not able to get up and go into the water. He must have been brought there by someone else, maybe on a regular basis. Some Greek manuscripts do not contain the last part of verse 3, "waiting for the moving of the waters," and all of verse 4 which speaks of an angel coming regularly to stir the water. There those who stepped into it first were healed of their malady.

We are not told how old the man was Jesus talked with. Nor do we know his name. We are told though he was "in his sickness thirty-eight years" (v. 5). When Jesus saw him, the man was lying down which probably indicates he was paralyzed. Also, from what Jesus said to the crippled man later, after Jesus had healed him, implies rather strongly that his problem was caused by sin in his life. Jesus did say to him, "Do not sin anymore, so that nothing worse may befall you" (v. 14).

The man there under one of the cloisters had his affliction for thirty-eight years (v. 5). Imagine not to be able to walk for that long. That's bad enough, but add to that the horrible letdown, the disappointment he faced time after time as he came there to be healed and had to be carried home no better than when He came.

This then was the occasion and setting for this portrait of Jesus pursued by killers. What next? It is the miracle. Jesus healed this dear man on the spot. And He did so simply by the spoken word. And He did it, according to the text, without screaming at him or striking him as so many self-professed "healers" do today.

Jesus knew the plight of this man and exactly how long he had his paralysis. He did not need anyone to tell Him. As the Son of God, He knew all things past, present, and future about all people everywhere. His was and is a supernatural knowledge. The question Jesus asked the man does sound a little strange and at first seems unnecessary. However, ever thirty-eight years it would not be surprising that one may have at times given up. Jesus asked him, "Do you want to get well?" Without knowing or probably caring who was speaking to him, the man in need answered with a sad complaint. "No one has ever tried to help me when I try to get into the water", he said. "In fact, they always rush ahead of me" (v. 7), he added.

Immediately, Jesus responded by telling him to get up, pick up his pallet, and walk (v. 8). What a bold request that was for one who had not walked for thirty-eight years. But the disabled man did exactly what Jesus told him to do. He did it immediately without any prodding or repeating of the instruction. Though not a problem with Jesus or with the healed man, what both had done was a big problem for the Jewish leaders who either witnessed the miracle or were told about it. The incident took place on the Sabbath. That was their problem

In the minds of the Jews, both Jesus and the healed man had violated the fourth commandment, "Remember the sabbath day, to keep it holy" (Exodus 20:8). The Jewish leaders who were already trying to find some fault with Jesus, trying to trap Him, had added much to the law of Moses. What they added, in time, became just as authoritative as the law itself for them and the people in general. Both Jesus and the healed man probably did violate the tradition of the Jews, but neither of them had violated the true meaning of the law God gave Moses.

The Murmuring Jews' Response to the Miracle, vv. 10–18

It seems that the Jews, a specific group of leaders, did not let the man who had just been miraculously and marvelously healed walk very far before they approached him. They did so not to rejoice with him at what Jesus had done. Oh no, they only wanted to accuse him of carrying his pallet on the Sabbath (v. 10). He was not at all concerned about what day of the week it was now that he could walk. No longer would he ever have to come hoping for someone to help him get into the water as he had done for years and years. He was healed! He could walk. He could even carry his pallet!

Without hesitation, the healed man told his accusers that whoever it was who healed him told him to pick up his pallet and walk. In other words, he was not about to quibble with the Jews over what day it was. What he really did in his response was tell the Jews to go away, find the One who healed him and air their scrupples with Him (v. 11).

It seems these accusing Jews pretended they did not know who it was who told the cripple to get up, pick up his pallet, and walk. Truthfully, the one-time cripple told them he did not know who it was. We can almost see him turning away then from the Jews and joyfully maybe even jogging away from them. Maybe as he was leaving, he turned his head back and said, "I really don't know who told me that." There was a large crowd there and Jesus had slipped away on purpose.

Very likely, after seeing the paralyzed man get up and walking and carrying what he had been lying on, Jesus went to the temple and even there looked for him. He found the man and approached him. We must remember this one-time cripple did not know who had spoken to him and enabled him to walk. Jesus said to His friend, "Behold you have become well" (v. 14). But He did not stop with that. He went on to tell the man to go and sin no more. And Jesus added, "So that nothing worse may befall you." These words from Jesus seem to imply that the man's physical handicap may have been the result of some sinful behavior.

The walking miracle went away and told the Jews, probably the same ones who had come to him before, that Jesus had performed the miracle. Ah, the Jews now had the excuse they were looking for to persecute Jesus. Little did these people care whether or not the handicapped man walked. It is in fact obvious they did not care about him at all. As far as they were concerned, Jesus had violated the law according to their tradition. He had not only worked on the sabbath but told His convert to work also on the sabbath.

Jesus' answer to the Jews who were persecuting Him was, "My Father is working until now and I myself am working" (v. 17). This statement angered them even more and resulted in more heated persecution of Jesus. Jesus called God, in His reply, His Father. They took that to mean He was making Himself equal with God (v. 18). And they were right. That is precisely what He intended to do because, in fact, He and God the Father were and are of the same divine essence or nature. Verse 18 is key to understanding this portrait.

Jesus had an altogether unique relationship with God. He was the "only begotten," the unique, the one and only of a kind, Son of God (3:16). Believers in the Lord Jesus Christ as the Substitute for their sins become sons and daughters of God in His heavenly family. But Jesus' Sonship does not mean He is merely in God's family. It means He is totally equal in deity with the Father.

God the Father continues to work on the Sabbath as He has always done, Jesus said. Since He is equal in nature with God, He too is free to work the work of God whenever and wherever He chooses. What He chooses to do is always right and is always in harmony with God's law whether or not it is in harmony with any of the traditions the Jews have added to that law.

Jesus' claim to have God as His Father infuriated these Jews beyond description. This caused them to seek even more to kill Him. Why? Because they got His message. Indeed He was making Himself equal with God, v. 18).

Personal Applications

Jesus gave the people around Him every opportunity to believe in Him, to accept Him as God's remedy for their sin. We have seen from every angle of this portrait examples of Him doing this. He healed the man who could not walk, not only to help him walk but to demonstrate to him and all around him that He was all He claimed to be.

Gazing at this portrait should cause us to think about whom we can help along life's way. Do we run ahead of those less fortunate than we are? Do we who are not handicapped park in the spot for those who are handicapped? Often, we do not mean to do this but without thinking we fail to offer a hand to the needy. Why not start looking for opportunities to do this? It may open a door for telling someone about Jesus who though pursued by killers was compassionate and helpful.

Study Questions

1. What was the portrait of Jesus we looked at before this one?

2. How does this one we saw here compare with that one?

3. Why do you think Jesus chose to minister to the man who could not walk?

4. How did the Jews respond to the miracle Jesus performed?

5. What was the difference between the response of the healed man and that of the Jews to Jesus' miracle?

Equal with God

Portrait 7

John 5:19–47

A MAN WHO had not walked for thirty-eight long years was healed by Jesus. As we have seen in John's sixth portrait, Jesus healed him on the Jewish Sabbath day. A group of Jews who were determined to not only oppose Him also wanted to kill Him. They thought they had caught Jesus in a trap. In their way of thinking Jesus had not only broken the Sabbath law, but He had also made Himself equal with God. For this reason, the Jews were emboldened to kill Jesus. Their law allowed them to do this to any mere human who claimed to be equal with God. Jesus, of course, was fully man, but He was also fully God. In the portrait before us we will see how He substantiated His claim to be equal with God.

Affirmations of Equality with God, vv. 19–24

God the Father ordained the plan He designed for His world. Jesus, God's only begotten Son, humbled Himself to become one of us and willingly and lovingly submitted Himself to that plan. Everything he did in His life on earth and in his death on the cross was in perfect harmony with His Father's plan (v. 19). Jesus was busy doing the work of God.

Jesus tried to assure His critics that God the Father loved Him and was very well pleased with what He was doing and would do. Always, Jesus was doing what His heavenly Father wanted Him to do and to say. Jesus the Son of God was all-powerful just as God the Father was. Both could do anything they chose to do which was in harmony with their nature.

As Jesus answered His critics, He told them that He, God's Son, could give life to the dead; He could raise the dead just as surely as His Father could (v. 21). That claim must have stunned those accusing Him. They, of course, would have known about Elijah and Elisha to whom God gave power to raise the dead. In both of these Old Testament cases, however, the power came only after the answer to specific prayer (1 Kings 17:17–24; 2 Kings 4:32–37). Jesus, by contrast, claimed to raise the dead when He chose to do so. He did this in fact three times during His sojourn here (Mark 6:41–42; Luke 7:14–15; John 11:43–44).

In addition to claiming all power as an affirmation of His being equal with God, Jesus also affirmed it by claiming to possess divine authority. The Father "has given all judgment to the Son," Jesus said (v. 22 cf. v. 27). The reason this awesome authority was given to Jesus is so that all would honor Him with the same honor they give to God. And then reminding His critics who were not giving Him any honor but were in fact trying to kill Him, Jesus told them of the awful consequences of not honoring Him. He said, "He who does not honor the Son does not honor the Father who sent Him" (v. 23). Furthermore, those who believe in Him have eternal life. Those who do not believe remain in a state of spiritual death and will face the judgment of God (v. 24). Here again He was claiming to be equal with God. Would those who pursued Him to kill Him ever believe Jesus was who He claimed to be? Did they ever have second thoughts about their evil intent?

Activities of Equality with God, vv. 25–29

The first activity Jesus referred to as He continued to answer His critics was that in the future the dead would hear His voice and live. Jesus gave spiritual life, eternal life, to all who received Him as their Savior. Also, He promised to raise the dead in the future. In both the physical and spiritual sense He claimed to be the Life-giver. They knew full well what Jesus was claiming by his assertions—He was equal with God. After all, they too believed only God could give life and raise the dead. The key verse to help us remember this portrait is verse 26.

Second, Jesus said He had been given authority to execute judgment upon mankind in the future. He had this right because He is equal with God in His divine nature.

The third, activity demonstrating Jesus' equality with God was His ability to raise the dead. Some, He said, would be raised to a resurrection of life and others to a resurrection of judgment. Jesus was not teaching that both of these resurrections would occur at the same time. Rather, His point was that both believers and unbelievers would be raised and He would be involved in both of these resurrections. Both are, of course, still future certainties.

Acclamations of Equality with God, vv. 30–47

Can you imagine how these critics of Jesus might have responded to His affirmations and activities of equality with God? Surely, they would not have been silent as they heard all these things. They must have been grumbling and complaining to each other, perhaps even trying to interrupt Jesus, to show their total rejection of what He was saying. Based on what we know from the rest of Scripture, they went away the same as they came to Him—in unbelief.

Jesus expressed His complete reliance upon the One who had sent Him to this world. His own will was always in perfect accord with God the Father's will. It was Jesus' goal to always do the will of His heavenly Father.

In John 5:30–47 there are four testimonies, or we might call them acclamations, of Jesus' equality with God. Before giving these four Jesus made what might be misunderstood as a strange and perplexing statement. He said, "If I alone bear witness Myself, My testimony is not true? (v. 31). He did not mean by this that His witness of Himself, His claims, were false. No, they were all perfectly valid.

Rather, what he did mean was, as He stood there in front of His critics, that contrary to a court of law where one's personal testimony would be biased, His was totally unbiased. This was true because of all He had already told them. And, the four witnesses he was about to give verified and fully agreed with His claims.

John the Baptist gave clear testimony to Jesus' equality with God (vv. 33–35). These very same Jews before Jesus had heard the Baptist's call of the Jews to repentance and His declaration, "Behold the Lamb of God who takes away the sin of the world (1:29). Also, there can be no doubt they heard him say he was not the Messiah but was His forerunner. "He must increase but I must decrease " must have come to their minds many times. There was no mistaking what John meant when he said that Jesus was "the Son of God" (1:34).

These bent on getting rid of Jesus also knew how much the Jewish people at large respected John the Baptist. They had also to contend with these people if they should succeed in killing Jesus. John had a large following, many gathered to hear him and many responded to his message, "Repent for the kingdom of heaven is at hand."

Apparently, Jesus' critics on this occasion went to consult with John and he told them the truth about Jesus. It would be hard for the Jews to receive only part of what he preached. After all, these people had responded positively to John's message. They even rejoiced for a time in the light John had brought them

The next acclaim or witness which Jesus made in defense of His being equal with God was the witness of His own works (v. 36). The "works" Jesus said He did were works given to Him by God the Father. These many works, He said, send forth loud proclamation that He was indeed sent by the Father. Thus "works" show the character of the one who performs them.

These "works" seem to be a reference to the miracles Jesus performed. The Jews to whom He was speaking had already been made aware of His miracle-working power. There was the water-into-wine miracle (chap. 2). Then the healing of the nobleman's son (chap. 4). The miracle of healing at the pool of Bethesda (5:1–18) was another mighty miracle. These and the miracles Jesus would perform later were a great testimony than even John gave. These works of His were given to Him by the Father according to His own testimony (5:36).

Then came the acclaim of God the Father of His Son Jesus (vv. 37–38). The evidence was mounting and His critics must have been squirming. Jesus' heavenly Father was the God of the Old Testament Scriptures. They knew very well whom Jesus was referring to as His Father, the One who had sent Him. At Jesus' baptism at the hands of John, God the Father's voice was heard: "This is my beloved Son in whom I am well please" (Matthew 4:17). Also as Jesus told the Jews a number of times their Old Testament gave testimony that He was equal with God.

A sharp piercing word was uttered by Jesus to His accusers. That word was that they did not have God's Word abiding in them because they did not believe His Father—God—who had sent Him into the world. Unbelief, in other words, was the reason they did not have eternal life. That always has been the reason why people will be eternally separated from God.

Fourthly, Jesus said the Scriptures gave acclaim, gave witness, that He was equal with God (vv. 39–47). What this really means is that Jesus—the Living Word of God—and the Bible—the Written Word of God—both testify to the full deity of Jesus Christ.

What would the Jews do with this acclaim from Jesus? What could they say about it since they and He both believed the Old Testament Scriptures were the Word of God.

Jesus continued His piercing remarks to His accusers. Their attitude toward the Scriptures, He told them, was that they thought in them they had eternal life (v. 39). Yet, several times in His discourse with them He told them eternal life would come only to those who placed their faith in Him. At first glance it appears that Jesus was saying the Jews were wrong in thinking the Scriptures gave direction on how to gain eternal life. Instead, He said they were wrong in thinking just because they were students of Scripture, they therefore had eternal life. Their problem was they had not searched the Scriptures correctly. If they had, they would have seen how the Scriptures pointed to Jesus as the Savior.

The Old Testament Scriptures were quoted and referred to often by Jesus. He affirmed the full inspiration of the Old Testament and therefore also its authority. He in fact called even small portions of Scripture the very Word of God. There are literally dozens and dozens of times when Jesus appealed to the Scriptures then available when rebuking sin and when comforting His people.

Only the Old Testament part of our Bible was written when Jesus was here on earth and He used it extensively in His ministry. Near the end of His life on earth Jesus made provision for the New Testament. Before He left His disciples, He told them He had many more things to teach them but they were not able to know them at that time (16:12). They were promised divine guidance into other truths to be given by the Holy Spirit after His departure (15:26–27; 16:13). Furthermore, Jesus promised His disciples the aid of the Spirit in what they would say. The Spirit, He said, would teach them and cause them to remember the things He taught them (14:27).

Jesus knew the Old Testament far better even than the Jews who studied it daily and could quote large portions of it from memory. Yet these Jews whom Jesus was talking to had missed Him in the Scriptures. They therefore missed the only way of salvation through Him. They were simply unwilling to come to Him for salvation (v. 40). They refused to come, no doubt, because they were self-righteous and saw no need for His salvation. That, by the way, is why many today do not come to Jesus. They think they are doing the best they can and do not need Jesus. Their hope is that in the end the good they do will outweigh the bad. How sad!

The criticism of these Jews continued. They did not have the love of God in them, Jesus said. They stubbornly refused to receive Him even though He came in His Father's name. They received glory from each other. We would say they patted each other on the back but adamantly refused to seek God's glory (v. 44).

Jesus concluded His acclamations of equality with God by reminding the Jews that even Moses who was highly revered by them accused them. They had set their hopes on Moses. He was their hero, their savior. Jesus told them they really did not believe everything Moses wrote. If they had, they would have believed Jesus because Moses wrote of Him. Jesus concluded with, "If you do not believe his writings, how will you believe My words?" (v. 47).

Personal Applications

How is it with you? Do you believe that Jesus is equal with God, that He is just as much God as God the Father is?

Since Jesus possesses divine authority equal with God's authority, we need to acknowledge it and submit ourselves, place ourselves under His authority in our daily lives. In short, that means we need to live according to Scripture. We are exhorted to do this, but not so we can earn salvation or work to keep it, but because we have it.

When the Lord Jesus Christ is received as the Substitute for our sins, He becomes our Savior and wants to be our Lord as well. Someone is on the throne of our lives; either God is or we are. Many of us want to be on the throne ourselves without any concern for God unless, of course, some awful tragedy befalls us, our family, or even our friends. Then suddenly we want God to be in charge and bring healing or any other kind of help we may need at that time. Jesus the Son of God who is equal with God longs to be not only our Savior, but also our Lord.

Study Questions

1. In this portrait of Jesus what do we see Him doing that demonstrates He is equal with God?

2. Who was Jesus speaking to as this portrait developed?

3. From whom did Jesus say His power came?

4. What are the four testimonies to Jesus' equality with God?

5. What steps could you take this week to be more submissive to God, to make Him Lord of your life? You might be surprised if you start making a list.

Provision and Protection

Portrait 8

John 6:1–21

COME UP close so you can see clearly this portrait of Jesus. Notice surrounding Him are many people. There seems to be a lot more men than women or children. I wonder why that is the case. The disciples are standing close by Jesus. They seem to be disturbed about something. Some of them look nervous and on edge. Why? Jesus is talking to them. Oh, there is Peter elbowing his way to Jesus. He is talking to Him. Now the large crowd is seated. They all seem to be very orderly. Let's look at the account of this incident in the Bible, John chapter 6. In this chapter we will witness two miracles performed by Jesus. One is on the land and the other on the sea.

The Miracle on the Land, vv. 1–15

John placed the time this miracle was performed as "after these things." He used this expression a number of times in his Gospel. It did not mean that what follows took place immediately after what had just happened. The phrase describes an indefinite length of time. In this case, he most likely was referring to the Passover Feast of one year before (5:1). That same Passover Feast was being observed when Jesus miraculously multiplied a little boy's lunch to feed over five thousand (6:4).

At the place where I grew up in Pennsylvania bread was called "the staff of life" by the older folks. All over the world bread does seem to be a staple food. People from various countries have different kinds, shapes, and textures of bread. Though high in carbohydrates, it has sustained life all over the world as perhaps no other single food item has done.

Luke's record of this same miracle (Luke 7:10) tells us the "other side of the sea" John referred to was the east side of the Sea of Galilee. This same body of water was earlier called Gennesaret and then later it was called Tiberias because a town by that name was built on its shore. The place where Jesus went on the other side of the Sea was a mountain near Bethsaida. He went there with His disciples to get some reprieve from the crowds following Him.

As the Son of God, Jesus knew, of course, what He would do there that would be of great benefit for the disciples and those who came there to receive His blessing and benefit.

Why were all these people following Jesus? Did they want to accept Him as their Savior? Did they wish to make public that He was their Lord? Probably, neither of these. John tells us they followed because they saw and probably heard how Jesus was healing the sick and even raising the dead. Naturally, all of us would be attracted to someone today who was not just claiming to do these things but was truly doing them before our very eyes. So we cannot fault those people for following Jesus for that reason.

From where Jesus and His disciples were on the mountain they could see the large crowd below. That is when Jesus said to Philip, "Where can we get bread to feed all these people?" He knew the people were tired and hungry and He knew too that before they could listen to Him and learn from Him, they needed to have food.

Why did Jesus ask this question of Philip? Did Jesus not know that He would perform a miracle there and satisfy the people's hunger? Of course, Jesus knew all about everything He, the disciples, and the people would do. This question to Philip was to put his faith to the test (v. 6).

Philip may or may not have been thinking about where they could go to buy bread for the crowd, which was the question first raised. He was from the area and would have known, most likely. Finances were on his mind. He said to Jesus "two hundred denarii" would not be anywhere near enough to feed them all even if each one ate only a small amount (v. 7). One denarius which was a Roman coin was worth what the common laborer would get for one day's wages.

Had Philip forgotten who Jesus was? Did he forget about His miracle-working power? How could he have forgotten so soon how Jesus turned water into wine? What about His healing the nobleman's son and the man who had not walked for thirty-eight years? It is easy, is it not, to ask such questions of someone else. But we too oftentimes forget what God has done for us in the past. Jesus has not changed. He is still the One with divine power and He can do "exceeding abundantly beyond all that we ask or think, according to the power that works in us" (Ephesians 3:20).

Andrew at least reminded Jesus about the small lad with five barley loaves of bread and two fish. But then he said in essence, What difference does that make? There's no way such a small lunch could feed this crowd. Maybe we can detect a little faith in Andrew's statement. It is almost as though he implied this: "But you can multiply that so there will be enough. We saw You perform other miracles just days ago."

Immediately after Andrew's word, Jesus said to him and all the others, "Have the people sit down" (v. 10). This meant they were to recline as they normally did to eat. The disciples did not hesitate or ask any more questions but somehow got the message to that large crowd. And they all sat down on the lush green grass. There were about five thousand men there besides women and children (cf. Matthew 14:21).

What an awesome sight that must have been. John does not tell us how they convinced the small boy to give his lunch to them or whether he gave his little lunch to Jesus himself. It seems there was an almost endless supply as Jesus took the loaves and the fish and distributed them to His disciples. Did the loaves and fish multiply as Jesus kept filling the baskets or did the baskets not even get empty as the people were fed? The disciples gave the miracle bread and fish to the people. Each person did not just have a small portion. No, they all ate all they wanted with some left over (v. 11). Let us make this the key verse for this portrait.

When Jesus was assured they all had all they wanted, He instructed His disciples to gather up all the leftovers (v. 12). He did not want any of the bread or fish to be wasted. Very likely the disciples and Jesus ate the food later.

Again, the disciples obeyed Jesus and gathered up what was left over after the crowd had eaten. Actually, there were twelve baskets filled with bread. The fish must have all been eaten (v. 13).

The result of what Jesus did for the people was that they said, "He must have been a prophet sent by God into the world." They had never before seen such a demonstration of divine power. In fact, some from the same crowd tried to take Jesus by force and hail Him as their King. They must have seen Him as the One who would deliver them from the Roman oppression under which they lived.

Indeed, Jesus did come to institute the Jews' kingdom promised to them by the prophets. But before that deliverance and His kingly reign, the Jewish leaders needed to repent and accept Him as their Savior-God, their Messiah. Jesus, therefore, withdrew Himself and went back up the mountain, there alone, no doubt, to pray (v. 15). Think of it, God the Son prayed. We will look later at Him doing just that.

The Miracle on the Sea, vv. 16–21

This miracle was performed later the same evening on the day the multitude was fed and filled as Jesus multiplied the five loaves and two fish. After that marvelous miracle Jesus sent the people away and went back to the mountain. It appears that He withdrew from the crowd because some wanted to take Him by force and make Him King. Perhaps, they decided to gather a revolt against the Roman rule. Matthew and Mark both refer to this incident and mention that Jesus sent the disciples away to the other side of the sea. It began to get dark or they waited thinking Jesus would soon come back down to the shore and meet them. After some time, they decided to leave for the other side. The breadth of the Sea of Galilee was six or seven miles. Storms came suddenly on that body of water because of the surrounding mountains. These would turn the calm sea into a very rough, foaming, and raging dangerous place to be. When the air cooled in the evening, it would rush down over the Sea and cause it to churn the water creating a foam. Often the wind came from the west. If it came from that direction on this occasion, the disciples had to row against it to get to the other side.

Even though these men knew the Sea and how rough it could become, they were very afraid. Some of these men had made their living in boats on this water. I am convinced Jesus ordered the high winds at that precise time so they would realize both His presence and His power. He performed a miracle. John tells us the sea was "stirred up" and a strong wind was blowing" (v. 18).

The miracle on the sea began when the disciples were made to come to the end of their resources. God often works the same way with us. Unless we are brought to the place where we cannot solve our problems, we often fail to trust God fully.

When exactly the storm came we are not told. We do know though that they were about half way across when they saw Jesus walking on the water. Most likely the storm began soon after they left the shore. Jesus came up close to the boat of frightened men. How did He calm them? He assured them He was the One who had called them to be His disciples. "It is I," He said. Maybe they thought that because He had called them, they would have a trouble-free life. Surely, they were not expecting such life-threatening experiences. They, like we, needed to learn that following Him did not mean life would become a bed of roses minus the thorns. Jesus never promised such a life to His followers.

The second thing Jesus said to the disciples was, "Do not be afraid" (v. 20). They could not hide their fear and frustration. In today's language it could be said that they were "scared to death." And Jesus knew that. They had been brought to the end of themselves. Their lives were in jeopardy. Storm or not, there was no longer reason to be afraid. When Jesus said, "It is I," He was reminding them He was claiming to be Jehovah God, the One who would never fail or forsake His own. They understood that and took comfort in it.

As soon as they were assured of whom this was walking up to their boat, the storm on the outside and the storm on the inside of these men ended. When He was received by them, the storm began to subside. John does not tell us that Jesus got into the boat but Matthew (14:32–33) and Mark (6:51) do tell us this. These two also tell us that when Jesus got into the boat, the wind and storm subsided.

That is not all that happened when Jesus got into the boat. We are told that "immediately the boat was at the land to which they were going" (v. 21). Another miracle was performed. We cannot help but wonder how that felt to the disciples in the boat.

As we stand back and take a closer look at this portrait of Jesus providing food and protection, we see five miracles He performed. *First*, He multiplied the loaves and fish. *Second*, He created the storm on the sea. *Third*, He walked on the water. *Fourth*, He stilled the storm on the Sea and the storm in the disciples. *Fifth*, the boat and all the passengers were at the same moment at the land where they had intended to go.

Personal Applications

Believing that Jesus died as our Substitute for sin is the first step of faith. When Jesus called and the disciples said yes, they took the first step of faith. They soon learned there were other steps to take in their Christian walk. Faith is strengthened through trials. Following Jesus does not make one immune to troubles and trials.

Jesus used His disciples to assist Him when He performed miracles. He could have fed the multitude without their help. But they were permitted to distribute the lunch Jesus provided. The little boy willingly gave his lunch. Jesus could have fed the people without the boy's lunch. Think of it. They were all on the stage, you might say, with Jesus, not just observing from a distance.

Fear needs to be exchanged for faith. Like those disciples in that boat, we all need to learn that with Jesus we can have peace on the inside even though there is turmoil on the outside. That is not an easy lesson to learn. We all need to work at that every time we enter a storm.

Study Questions

1. Why do you suppose Jesus did not make the bread and fish appear to each one without the disciples being involved?

2. What does the lad with the small lunch teach us?

3. How did the multitude respond to Jesus after they experienced His miracle-working power?

4. Name the miracles Jesus performed in this portrait.

5. What lessons do you think the disciples learned from the miracle on the water?

6. Did you learn any lessons from this portrait? What are they?

The Bread of Life

Portrait 9

John 6:22–71

A LARGE CROWD of people were very interested in Jesus, especially after He multiplied the little boy's lunch and fed over five thousand in our last portrait. When He performed the miracle, Jesus gave them bread to eat. It was material bread that satisfied their hunger. But He knew they, and all mankind, needed more than that kind of bread. They and everyone also need spiritual bread which only God can give.

In this portrait of Jesus He wanted to give the people spiritual bread. They did not really understand what He meant when He said He was the Bread of Life given by God from heaven. The main reason they followed Jesus so much was because they wanted Him to meet all their physical needs. They were indeed seeking Him but not for the most important reason.

We will observe, as we look closely at this portrait, realities to be learned and reactions from three groups to the miracle He performed.

Realities To Be Learned from a Miracle, vv. 22–40

First, let us be reminded what miracle Jesus performed that caused such a stir among the people. It was the feeding of five thousand men and surely some women and children. He fed them well with just five barley loaves and two small fish. Remember that after Jesus and His disciples fed the people, they went to the other side of the sea to Capernaum.

The next day the crowd Jesus had fed went where He and the twelve had been but Jesus and His disciples were not there. A group, presumably representing the larger crowd, decided to cross over the sea to Capernaum to look for Jesus. They did find Him there. "Rabbi, when did you get here?" they asked (v. 25). He did not tell them how or when He got there or why He was there.

What He did say to them must have puzzled them greatly. It was as though He read their minds and knew their true motive for seeking after Him. You seek me out, not because you saw a miracle performed but because you had your needs met (v. 26). Physical bread is necessary for survival but the need for spiritual food is even more important because it "endures to eternal life" (v. 27). The first reality to be learned then was the insufficiency of material bread.

Jesus knew there was strong opposition to what He was saying about Himself as bread from heaven. Four times in the description of this portrait Jesus said, "Truly, truly" (vv. 6, 32, 47, 53). This term repeated twice each time brings a special urgency and importance to what follows. After all, Jesus did say God the Father had placed His seal upon Him. A seal in that day was a guarantee of whatever it was upon.

The second reality to be learned from the miracle concerned the work of God (vv. 28–29). Spokesman for those who insisted on being where Jesus was responded to Jesus' admonition about working for the food which endures to eternal life (v. 27). They asked Him what they needed to do to work the works of God. The Savior's answer was that the work of God was to believe in Him (v. 28). These followers had not yet learned that. No doubt, they were thinking about the Mosaic law and something they may have missed. No, Jesus was not talking about any rule or ritual that would bring eternal life. The only "work" necessary to be made right with God was to "believe in Him whom He has sent" (v. 29).

Third, came the reality from the manna from heaven (vv. 30–36). Why would these people ask for a sign, a miracle, from Jesus before they would believe in Him? What about the miraculous feeding of the five thousand the day before? Truly, their minds were blinded. Surely, they did not think Jesus did not know about the supply of manna for the Jews during their wilderness journey.

Moses and the law given by him was so central in their minds that they could not think of anything else. Jesus reminded them Moses did not supply the manna from heaven for their fathers. God, His Father, did. He supplied the true bread for them in His own Person (v. 33). When they heard that they got very excited and said, "Give us this bread" (v. 34). "I am the Bread of Life, he who comes to Me shall not hunger, and he who believes in Me shall never thirst" (v. 35), He told them. Sadly, He also told them they had seen and heard Him, yet they had not believed in Him.

Fourth, was the reality still to be learned about the will of God the Father (vv. 37–40). Jesus wanted those questioning Him to know all who believed on Him were gifts given to Him by the Father. They needed to know His heavenly Father was definitely involved in the salvation of sinners. Those who come to Him, Jesus said, He would indeed receive, He would most certainly not cast out (v. 37).

To do His Father's will was His highest goal, Jesus said. He did not come to earth reluctantly. But willingly He came; He was born of Mary, became one of us to do only the Father's will. The Father did send Him (3:16) but not against Jesus' own will or desire.

What exactly was the Father's will in sending His Son? It was that He might be the Substitute and provide the substitution for sin. Also, a part of the Father's will was that all who accepted Jesus as the One who paid the debt they owed would never be lost (v. 39). Jesus, the spiritual Bread of life, the very Son of God, when received would give that person "eternal life" (v. 40).

Some of the same people who were fed miraculously by Jesus the day before must have been reminded how the disciples of Jesus took up twelve baskets full after all had been fed. He did not want any of the miracle-lunch to be lost or wasted. Surely they remembered this when Jesus told them none, not even one, who believed on Him would ever be lost spiritually. Even physical death would not separate them from Him. He would, in fact, raise them up on the last day" (vv. 39–40).

People often are afraid to place their faith, their trust, in Jesus. Why is that? It is often because they are scared that they will not be able to "hold out." Maybe they will commit some great sin and then lose their salvation. This is sad. Truth is, since salvation is a gift from God and cannot be earned, neither can it be lost by the person doing or not doing anything. The gift of God is eternal life. To be sure, sin brings consequences. God wants His people to live for Him but eternal life will never become terminal life.

Reactions to the Discourse of Jesus, vv. 41–71

The reactions to what Jesus taught were varied. There were three distinct reactions from those who heard what He said. Interestingly, the same responses are given today when people learn about Jesus.

First, was the reaction of the Jews (vv. 41–59). These people referred to as "the Jews" (v. 41) were the same group of Jews who responded so vehemently to Jesus' healing the man who had not walked for thirty-eight years (5:10). They doubtlessly represented the religious rulers over the Jews. Up until this time they were not mentioned. How they got where Jesus was or even knew where He was we are not told.

We are told though that once again they opposed what Jesus was saying and doing. They "were grumbling about Him." Why? Because He said He was the Bread from heaven. After all, they reasoned in their unbelief, we know Joseph and Mary to whom He belongs. How could He therefore say truthfully He came down out of heaven? These Jews saw Jesus with their physical eyes, but they had never seen Him with eyes of faith. That is why they had not believed in Him.

Knowing what they were doing, Jesus said to them, "Do not grumble among yourselves" (v. 43). He then proceeded to tell them what they surely had heard Him say before. First, He told them God the Father draws people who when they come to Him receive eternal life. But they cannot have that life unless they come to Him.

Second, Jesus reminded the Jews that no one has ever seen God in all His fulness except Him. Pointedly, He said to them that no one can have eternal life who does not believe in Him and He is the Bread of Life (v. 48). This is our key verse. The bread or manna their fathers ate did not spare them from death. They ate and died. In stark contrast, all who partake of Him, the heavenly Bread, will never die spiritually (vv. 49–50).

Once again Jesus said to these religious but lost people unless they would eat of Him, that is believe in Him, they would not have eternal life. Eating was a figure of speech Jesus used to explain how eternal life was given to those who believed. This analogy is used by Jesus in verses 50-58 of John 6. First, "the Jews" grumbled to each other about Jesus and what He was saying (v. 41). Then they soon "argued" with each other about how Jesus could give His flesh to them to eat (v. 52).

Jesus used specifics in His words to His critics. The tense He used with the verb "eat" in verse 50 makes clear He was talking about the initial reception of Jesus as Substitute for sin, a single act, not an ongoing process. The second word used in verse 54 is not only a different word but a different tense as well. The meaning here is an ongoing eating, in this case a process of eating on Jesus as the Living Bread. The contrast between material bread and the spiritual bread of Jesus is made repeatedly in His confrontation with the Jews.

The followers of Jesus, who are called His disciples (v. 60), overheard what He told "the Jews." They too needed some help in understanding what Jesus meant by some of His teaching. No doubt, some among them had truly believed in Jesus but still wanted more help. Many, perhaps most, of these people who saw Jesus' miracles on the other side of the Sea and followed Him to Capernaum were not genuine believers. They were curious though. Just like "the Jews," they did not get it. They were very confused. The fact of the matter is, they "grumbled" to each other about what Jesus had said to "the Jews" (v. 61).

The Savior knew all about their grumbling, and He let them know He did. He reminded these followers that if they would continue on with Him until He ascended back to heaven, maybe then they could be assured. He did, in fact, come from heaven. Too, they were told the Spirit was the One who gave life through the Bread of heaven (v. 63).

Jesus also knew who among these followers believed in Him and who did not (v. 64). He even knew who would betray Him. Many of Jesus' followers decided they did not want to be His disciples, His followers, any longer. They "withdrew" from Him and stopped "walking with Him" (v. 66).

After many deserted Jesus, He turned to the twelve He had called to follow Him. It seems He expressed real sorrow for those who turned their backs on Him. To the twelve who were His disciples in a special sense He said, "You do not want to go away also, do you?" (v. 67). All of these men had been chosen by Him. He needed all of them. Admittedly, they were a rather motley crowd. There was impetuous Peter, doubting Thomas, materialistic Philip, fiery John, tax collector Matthew, and betrayer Judas. Jesus truly loved all of them.

When we look into the mirror, we often ask, "how could Jesus love Me with all my faults and failures?" Thankfully, He always hates sin but loves sinners. God did not choose to bestow His grace on us because we deserved it or because we were lovely. The truth is He loved us in spite of our lost hopeless condition and He still does and always will.

Impetuous Peter spoke for the rest in response to Jesus' question. He said these beautiful words, "To who shall we go? You have the words of life" (v. 68). Peter went on to speak for the others when he said, "We have believed and have come to know that You are the Holy One of God" (v. 69).

A rather sad word was added to Peter's testimony of faith. Jesus responded to it by saying He did indeed choose the twelve. But one among them would turn out to be His betrayer (vv. 70–71). This was said a year before Judas actually did betray Him. Jesus described His betrayer as "a devil." The word speaks of one hostile to Him, an enemy, a slanderer. John the apostle added the identification of Judas as the betrayer to whom Jesus referred (v. 71). Judas Iscariot played the part of a believer very well. But he was not genuine. His sad example should cause us to be sure we are for real.

Personal Applications

We too have lessons to learn, do we not? It is easy to point out lessons which others should learn. But we often fail to acknowledge that we also need to be continually learning. For example, do we really live our lives as though we believed material things do not bring to us what we need most—peace and contentment. Have we learned yet that God's work is far more important than ours? Are we proud that we believed or are we thankful? How do we respond to biblical teaching that brings conviction to us?

Study Questions

1. What miracle formed the basis for this portrait of Jesus?

2. What realities did those who witnessed that miracle need to learn?

3. How did "the Jews" react to Jesus' discourse?

4. How did many of the followers of Jesus respond?

5. How do you plan to put something you learned from looking at this portrait of Jesus into practice today?

Surprise Visit to the Temple

Portrait 10

John 7

WHY A surprise visit to the temple? For whom was it a surprise? As we look carefully at this portrait, we see many people there. Among them are the half-brothers of Jesus, boys Mary and Joseph had after the miraculous conception and birth of Jesus. The people who had come to Jerusalem for the annual Feast of Tabernacles celebration were divided over what to think of Jesus. Some insisted He was a good man; others said, No, He is not good because He has brought division among us. All over the place, there were groups of Jews grumbling and arguing with each other about Jesus.

This portrait of Jesus introduces us to the period of increased conflict in the life of Jesus. His enemies were determined to kill Him, and they became more intense and antagonistic in their pursuit. We need to keep in mind that the Jewish people at large were not trying to kill Him, though there were mixed reactions over Him. The Gentiles were not out to get Him either. It was the Jewish religious leaders who hated Him and pursued Him wherever He went.

This true story starts in Jesus' home with His half-brothers trying to persuade Him to go with them to Jerusalem to celebrate the Feast of Tabernacles. This Feast had some other names which were very descriptive of the event. We will get a peak at these later as we gaze at this portrait of Jesus.

Jesus and His Half-brothers, vv. 1–13

It may come as a surprise to some to know that Jesus lived in a divided home. That is, not all in the family were believers, all had not accepted Him as their Messiah and personal Savior. Matthew tells us the names of His brothers—James, Joseph, Simon, and Judas (not Iscariot) (Matthew

13:55). Jesus had sisters also, Matthew said (Matthew 13:56). All the brothers and sisters were born to Joseph and Mary after Jesus was born. He was Mary's firstborn son (Luke 2:7). Furthermore, she was a "virgin until she gave birth" to Jesus (Matthew 1:25).

Some insist that Jesus' "brothers" (John 7:3) were His cousins. There is, however, no good substantial reason to take "brothers" in any other than its normal meaning.

The occasion which brought about Jesus' surprise visit in the temple is given in verses 1 and 2 and was threefold. First, He went from Judea north to Galilee to escape those who were determined to kill Him, and He did not want to incite a revolution among the people. Second, it was time for the Feast of Tabernacles, or Booths. This Feast was held at harvest time and the people who came encamped around the city in tents or in rather crude shelters which they erected. The entire event was to remind the people of the forty years of wandering in the wilderness which their parents had endured. Third, Jesus was in complete dependence upon the Father and His timing. He delayed going so that He would arrive at the precise time ordained of God the Father.

Jesus' brothers, or really half-brothers, urged Him to go to Jerusalem presumably with them, though they did not say that (v. 3). The reason they gave for this was "that your disciples may behold your works." Jerusalem was the big city, and there Jesus would have a larger audience to display His miracle-working power, they reasoned. These "brothers," it appears, never questioned the reality of Jesus' miracles. But they had not yet believed in Him as the Messiah promised in the Old Testament. They were not believing in Him, John tells us (v. 5).

Perhaps the half-brothers were even being a bit sarcastic as they pressed Jesus to go to the Feast. They may even have been thinking Jesus would get caught in a trap set by the religious authorities there. We simply do not know for sure what these men had in mind.

Very likely, they did not understand and therefore did not accept Jesus' response to them. My time to go is not now, He told them. He reminded them that He was following His heavenly Father's timetable. In this He differed from them. After all, He reminded them, He was hated by the world, but they were not hated. The world of mankind hated Him because He pointed out how unbelieving they were. His message convicted them and hardened them in their sin.

So Jesus stayed in Galilee, and His "brothers" went to the Feast in Jerusalem as He had told them to do (v. 8). The Feast lasted seven days, and then a special Sabbath followed. Since Jesus began His teaching in the temple in the middle of the celebration, it appears that He delayed leaving Galilee for a few days before going to the Feast. He followed His Father's timing. His half-brothers were there from the beginning of the Feast.

The Jews who represented the religious hierarchy in Jerusalem were looking for Jesus. They no doubt saw His "brothers" and insisted on knowing where He was. Can you guess why they wanted to see Him so badly? Was it because they wanted to encourage Him in His work? Absolutely not.

The general populace must have found out at least something about what the authorities thought about Jesus and had in mind concerning Him. The "multitudes" (v. 12) at any rate were "grumbling" about Him. Two contrasting views prevailed among them. Some said He was a good man. They were at least favorably disposed toward Him. Others, however, said He was not a good man and was leading the people astray (v. 12). These groups "grumbled" among themselves and did not make their views known openly because they feared the Jews who were trying to find Him (v. 13).

Jesus Teaching in the Temple, vv. 14–39

The Feast celebration lasted eight days. In about the middle of the Feast, Jesus entered the temple and began to teach (v. 14). We should never forget this key verse for this portrait. There would certainly have been many people in the temple as well as all around it. Jesus did not need to teach very long before those who listened were totally shocked by His performance. They could not believe their ears. They knew He had never been to any of their celebrated schools, yet He excited in them both amazement and admiration. They were stunned too at His knowledge of their Old Testament Scripture as well as the oral tradition surrounding it.

Upon hearing their question and knowing how puzzled they were, Jesus answered it even though they never asked Him but asked each other. "My teaching," Jesus said "did not originate with me. It isn't mine but came from the One who sent Me into the world." He never taught anything contrary to His heavenly Father's will. Once again, He was showing that He was equal with God and had been sent by Him.

All who were willing to do God's will would know His teaching was from God, Jesus told them (v. 17). Those who speak on their own authority and have not been sent by God seek their own glory. Jesus was not doing that. It was His desire that His Father would receive all the glory (v. 18).

The next part of Jesus' answer to the Jews who could not understand how He knew so much and expressed it all so well is in two parts. Both parts related directly to the law of Moses. First, He reminded them how that law said, "You shall not murder" (Exodus 20:13). This was the sixth commandment and they all knew it very well. He told them none of them obeyed the law fully. Why then, "Do you seek to kill me?" He asked them (v. 19). That was more than they could take. They accused Him of being demon possessed and that demon was trying to kill Him. This response shows that the Jews at large probably did not know that their leaders really were seeking to kill Him.

Second, Jesus told them how contradictory it was for them to say a male could be circumcised on the Sabbath and the law would not be broken, yet He healed a man on the Sabbath and because of it He was being pursued by killers.

Finally, it began to dawn on some of those gathered there that Jesus, it seemed to them, was being sought so they could kill Him (v. 25). There He was teaching publicly and no one laid hands on Him. "The rulers do not know that this is the Christ, do they?" they asked (v. 26). This statement seems to imply that many thought the rulers did not really know who Jesus was. If they had known it, they would not be trying to kill Him, they reasoned. This appears to have been an attempt to let the Jewish rulers off the hook, so to speak.

The crowd was not so convinced of who Jesus was either. They insisted they knew Jesus was from Bethlehem and grew up in Nazareth. However, a tradition developed that when Messiah would come, no one would know where He was from. So this tradition and their knowledge seemed to tell them that Jesus was not the Messiah. They were very confused. What about their Scripture which predicted Jesus would be born in Bethlehem (Micah 5:2 cf. Matthew 2:1)? Had they forgotten about this definite prophecy?

Jesus did not hesitate to tell the people in the temple that they did not know the true God. They knew Jesus and His claims to have come from God and not of Himself, but their knowledge did not lead them to accept Him as their Sin-bearer and Messiah (vv. 28–29). Those who asked the question, "How has this man become learned, having never been educated?" (v. 15) probably did not expect the answer they got. If the truth be known, they may have even regretted asking the question.

The official Jews, and no doubt some from the multitude who joined them, took decisive measures to seize Jesus. His claim to be Israel's Messiah and His bold statement that they did not even know God were all they could take. Yet, no one "laid hands on Him (v. 30). Why? Because His hour appointed by the Father had not yet come.

Furthermore, a good number of people from the multitude were becoming convinced that He was, in fact, the promised Messiah. Word of this got to the Pharisees. They, along with the chief priests, sent officers to take Jesus by force (vv. 31–32).

His crucifixion, resurrection, and ascension back to the Father were realities on Jesus' mind. In essence He said, "I will be here a short while longer, then I will return to the One who sent Me here. After I leave you will continue seeking Me but you won't find Me. And furthermore where I'm going you can't come" (vv. 33–34). As usual, this kind of talk startled the Jews and they began to try to figure what exactly He meant (vv. 35–36).

The Jews called the last day of the Feast of Tabernacles, the Great Day. It seems they referred to it that way because on this day their law said they were to abstain from work (Leviticus 23:39). The last day brought to an end their reading of the law which they were to do all week. Perhaps, it is thought, that on the last day it was customary for the priest to draw water from the Pool of Siloam. This vial of water was then taken to the temple, mixed with wine, and poured over the sacrifice on the altar.

Very likely, Jesus stood in the temple as this ceremony was going on and cried out His message of their coming to Him to have their thirst satisfied. Once again, He begged the people to come to Him for living water. John, the writer, then adds that Jesus was speaking about the coming of the Holy Spirit. He is the One those who believed on Jesus would receive in God's time (vv. 37–39).

The Multitudes Reactions, vv. 40–53

Those who heard Jesus were mystified. They tried to understand Him based on what they knew and had been taught. The reactions were varied therefore. Some acknowledged Jesus must be a prophet. Others said He was the Messiah indeed. And still others were bothered that He came out of Galilee. They were reminded that their Scripture predicted Messiah would be a descendant of David and come from Bethlehem (vv. 40–42).

As noted earlier, these lay people were right about Messiah coming from Bethlehem (Micah 5:2). What they must not have known or had forgotten was that Jesus was indeed born in Bethlehem. However, the Jewish leaders did know where Jesus was born and still rejected Him.

A great division arose among the people because of Jesus. There was no consensus as to how to respond to Jesus and His claims. There were some who wanted to capture Him and carry out the wicked aim of the official Jews. It was still not the hour appointed by God the Father for this to take place. Others were attracted to Jesus and felt that He possibly might be the Messiah.

The officers who had been sent to seize Jesus found themselves on the horns of a dilemma (v. 32). They were ordered to capture Jesus and bring Him to the chief priests and Pharisees. After listening to Him at length, they were so impressed and awestricken that they could not bring themselves to take Him. They returned emptyhanded to the ones who had given them the orders. The chief priests and Pharisees wanted to know, "Why did you not bring Him?" The officers had only one reason: "Never did a man speak the way this man speaks," they said. They had never heard such claims and defense of them before. These men had not placed their faith in Him, but they could not believe He was deserving of such hatred and death. In essence they had the same view as Pilate had later, "We find no fault in Him." The Pharisees asked, "Have you believed and been led astray also?" They wanted to know, "Have any of the Pharisees or rulers believed in Him?" (vv. 45–48).

The multitude does not really know the law, the Pharisees insisted. Then one of their own number spoke out and gave a short and straightforward lecture to the others. He was Nicodemus, by name the same one who came to Jesus by night (John 3). What he said implied that the Pharisees did not know fully the law either. The law does not judge a man without hearing him and knowing what he is doing, Nicodemus said. In other words, there is too much uncertainty here to judge this man.

With that said, the other Pharisees slandered Nicodemus by asking him if he was also a Galilean. Search the Scripture, they argued. Can you find any true prophet who came from Galilee. With that said, the Pharisees and the officers who did not complete their assignment all went to their homes. (vv. 50–53).

Personal Applications

This portrait shows the impossibility of being neutral when it comes to one's belief in Christ. The songwriter has put it well when he wrote, "Neutral you cannot be; some day your heart will be asking, 'What will He do with me?'" Either Jesus must be believed to have been sent from God and is fully equal with Him, the only true Substitute for sin, or rejected along with all His claims and testimony.

From the example of Nicodemus, we can learn how important it is to take a stand regardless how the majority feel or believe. Truth is costly.

We learn from the Pharisees in this portrait not to be so caught up in formalities and trivialities that we miss the true picture. They also unintentionally teach us that religion does not equip anyone for heaven. It is possible to be oh so religious and yet be lost. Jesus did not offer another way to God and heaven. He made very plain He was the only Way.

Study Questions

1. Who are the "brothers" in this portrait?

2. Why did Jesus not go up to the Feast with His brothers?

3. How was Jesus received when He got to the celebration?

4. What was the gist of Jesus' teaching in the temple?

5. Why did the Pharisees send officers to take Jesus?

6. Why did they not bring Jesus to them?

7. How has this portrait helped you understand Jesus better?

Light of the World

Portrait 11

John 8:1–21

IN THE New Testament all who have by faith received Jesus as their Substitute for sin are challenged to be lights in the world. Jesus said, "Let your light shine before men in such a way that they may see your good works, and glorify your Father who is in heaven" (Matthew 5:16).

As we will see in this portrait of Jesus, He claimed to be the Light of the whole world. His followers are to reflect His light. The better we know Jesus, the brighter will be our light.

The world truly needs the light, the testimony, of Jesus. It is full of darkness and needs the light of God's love and grace to shine in it. Throughout the Bible, darkness is often used to speak of sin and light is used to speak of holiness.

We will see, if we look closely, in this portrait the Light of the world not only exposing sin but also forgiving the sinner. Also, we will observe how Jesus silenced some of His fiercest critics.

Forgiving a Sinful Woman, vv. 1–11

Some do not believe John 7:53–8:11 is really a part of John's original Gospel. This is because some ancient manuscripts do not include these verses. They conclude therefore that these verses were added by a well-meaning copyist. However, there are several internal and external arguments that have been made for believing the passage is an authentic part of John's Gospel. There is every reason to believe that the same Pharisees involved at the close of chapter 7 are the ones Jesus debated in 8:13–21. Also, early church fathers considered the passage in question as authentic.

The woman in this passage was brought to Jesus by the scribes and Pharisees. Why? Were they interested in helping her? Were they hoping He could help her to leave her sinful lifestyle? No! The truth is they brought her to Jesus with ulterior motives. As was so often the case, they wanted to trick and trap Jesus. They wanted desperately to prove to the people He was not the One He claimed to be, Israel's Messiah and the world's Savior. In other words, they were using the woman as a means of finding fault with Jesus.

The specific occasion or setting for the story about this woman's encounter with Jesus came after Nicodemus reminded his Pharisee-friends that they were violating their law by rushing to judge Jesus. They then parted and went to their homes.

Jesus did not really have a home. He went to the Mount of Olives. The next morning He went into the temple again where He met with many people. He began to teach them. These were most likely many of the same people He taught there the day before.

Some scribes and Pharisees apparently went out and brought back with them a woman who reportedly had been caught in the act of adultery. Their trick question, "What do you say?" was prefaced with a reminder of what Moses commanded in Leviticus 20:10 and Deuteronomy 22:22–24. With their question, the Pharisees thought they had Jesus over a barrel, as the saying goes. But did they?

It is significant and interesting that the Pharisees brought scribes with them. This is the only time John mentions them in his Gospel. The scribes were the ones who copied the law and also taught it to the people. No doubt, they were brought along to strengthen their case against Jesus. They were not interested in anything but accusing Jesus. The pretense they made that they were deeply concerned with obeying the law was a farce. If that had really been their intent, they should have taken the woman to the Jewish authorities who could then have brought her to the established court. Why bring her to Jesus? What did they want Him to do about her? Oh, they failed also to bring the man with whom she had an adulterous relationship. According to the same law they used to accuse her, the man was also accused and to be punished.

Guided by the Spirit of God, John tells us they were testing Jesus with a view to accusing Him (v. 6). How did Jesus respond to His critics? Did He immediately proceed to answer them or to defend the woman? No, instead He stooped over and wrote in the sand. We do not know what He wrote, but that does not matter. What follows does matter very much.

After some time of pressuring Jesus by the people, He stood up straight and said to them, "He who is without sin among you, let him be the first to throw a stone at her" (v. 7). Having said that, He bent over again and continued writing in the sand.

It did not take long for the accusers to remember their other appointments. Beginning with the old men and then the younger ones, all the woman's accusers left Jesus and the woman (v. 9). Those gathered who witnessed the dialog apparently stayed.

Jesus then stopped writing in the ground and faced the accused woman. "Where are they?" He asked her (v. 10). "Has no one who was here condemned you?" She answered quickly, I'm sure. She said, "No one, Lord." Jesus then said to her, "Neither do I condemn you; go. From now on sin no more" (v. 11).

This account reminds me of a college class I attended as a guest. The professor was discussing how important he thought it was for us not to judge people's behavior. He appealed to this account to defend his point. "Even Jesus," he said, "did not condemn the woman brought to Him accused of committing adultery." He failed, however, to include in his remarks that Jesus did tell the woman to "go and sin no more." I could not restrain myself from making an observation. I raised my hand and said, "But didn't Jesus also tell the woman to go and sin no more?" This, of course, means He did view what she was accused of as sin. The professor gave a mild acknowledgment but then quickly went on with his lecture.

Just how are we to understand Jesus' response to the woman in this portrait? To begin, He clearly stated that she had sinned. He did not have or claim to have any civil authority to pursue judgment against her. The woman was brought to Jesus. She did not come on her own initiative. No doubt, as she listened to Jesus' response to her accusers, she was made to see her need of His forgiveness and cleansing and accepted Him as her Savior. Jesus condemned all sin, but He accepted the woman knowing her heart and forgave her and told her to stop the sin she was indulged in.

Silencing the Pharisees' Accusations, vv. 12–21

The caption over this portrait is "Light of the world" (v. 12). That makes this the key verse. Earlier, Jesus said, "I am the living bread" (6:51) and "I am the bread of life" (6:35). We have already looked carefully at that portrait of Jesus.

Above, we have noted how "the Light of the world" forgave a sinful woman who was brought to Jesus by His critics. Now let's look at this same Light of the world and observe how He shuts the mouths of those same critics again.

He does this first by His own testimony to them (vv. 12–18). His specific testimony to those Pharisees was that not only was He the Light of the world but also those who follow Him, that is, accept Him, would not walk or live in darkness any longer. They would no longer be in a state of lostness and hopelessness but would have Him as their Light of life.

The Pharisees did not like what He said. In fact, they were angry at Him for saying it. You are talking about yourself, they said. And they added, "What you are saying is not true. It is not worthy of acceptance; it is a lie" (v. 13). The law does indeed require two witnesses in criminal cases (Deuteronomy 17:6).

Jesus referred to this matter earlier (John 5:31–32). In that case, as here in this one, He appealed to His heavenly Father as witness alongside Himself. Take careful notice how Jesus responded to the horrible accusation the Pharisees had hurled against Him. First, He said that since He knew all things, His testimony should be received even if there would not be a second witness (8:14).

At the same time, Jesus told His opponents they did not know where He had come from or where He was going. They knew where He claimed to come from and where He claimed He was going, but they rejected His testimony; therefore, they did not really know. The Pharisees judged according to the flesh, the outward appearance (v. 15). These men were very determined not to accept Jesus as their Messiah and Substitute for sin. Their minds, therefore, were blinded to the truth. They judged according to the flesh completely and only. Jesus came to this world not to judge or condemn the world but that the world through Him might be saved (3:16).

Jesus was not violating the law by what He was doing and saying. He agreed with them on what it said (v. 17). His judgment or testimony was true. It was worthy to be received because along with His testimony there was also the testimony of His heavenly Father. There was no disparity between what Jesus said, what He claimed, and what His Father claimed about Him (v. 18). Of course, the Pharisees did not accept that Jesus had come from the Father and was equal to Him.

"Where is your Father?" they asked Jesus (v. 19). Jesus' answer was very specific. He said to them, "You don't know me, you don't accept me for who I am, and therefore you don't know my Father. If you knew me you would know my Father." No one can truly know God or even come to God who does not know and come through Jesus. He is the only way to God.

Since God the Father's time had not yet come, no one seized Jesus even though He had sharply rebuked Israel's Pharisees for their unbelief (v. 20). His final words to His critics on this occasion were straightforward. "I'm going away, you will seek Me but will not find Me," He said. "You will die in your sins," Jesus told the religious leaders of His day, "Where I'm going you cannot come" (v. 21).

Personal Applications

What a wonderful thing it is to know our sins are forgiven. Forgiveness does not remove all the consequences brought about because of sin. But it does mean those forgiven sins are no longer held against us. Imagine getting a notice along with a warning about how much you owe and the penalties attached if not paid by a specified time. Suppose too you do not have the money to pay and you know of no way to get the money. As you look at the bottom of the bill, you read, "The above has been paid in full by an anonymous friend." How wonderful! The company you owed no longer holds you accountable. Talk about relief!

When Jesus died in your place, He paid the debt you owed but could not pay. But that payment must be accepted before it will benefit you. Suppose in the above illustration you decided not to accept the payment made by someone else and you told the company you owed to return the check. The result would be that you then still owed the money. In the same way, God's gift of salvation must be received by faith or the sins are not forgiven.

Study Questions

1. Who brought the sinful woman to Jesus?

2. Why was she brought to Jesus?

3. What did Jesus tell those who brought her?

4. What did Jesus tell the woman?

5. What accusation did the Pharisees make against Jesus?

6. How did Jesus respond to them?

7. How can you benefit from this portrait of Jesus?

Great I Am

Portrait 12

John 8:22–59

THE PEOPLE to whom Jesus ministered responded differently to Him. In the portrait we are looking at now John gives us a second response to Jesus' forgiving the adulterous woman. The first response was from a minority of the onlookers who "believed in Him." The second response was from the delegates of Jews, sent by the Sanhedrin, to find fault in Him so that they could publicly discredit Him. They not only said they wanted to kill Him; they picked up stones to do just that—kill Him.

Look with me at this portrait of Jesus as the Great I Am. Let's walk slowly around it so we can see it from every angle John included in His portrait.

These days we all hear a lot of claims from religionists and those with no religious connections at all. People make boasting claims about themselves and about their products. We will see in the claims Jesus makes for Himself in this portrait that He defended them and demonstrated their truthfulness. He claimed as the Great I Am to be from heaven, to be the Son of God and the eternal One. And He was and still is all three today.

The Great I Am from Heaven, vv. 22–30

As we looked at the last portrait of Jesus, we saw Him teaching in the temple (v. 20). The religious elite were not at all sympathetic to Him or to what He said. The Pharisees wanted to seize Him but they did not. It was not the Father's time for Him to be taken and crucified. The last part of that portrait revealed how Jesus told His accusers they would die in their sin of unbelief. Where He was going, they could not come (v. 21).

This caused "the Jews" to say to each other, "Surely He will not kill Himself, will He?" (v. 22). It is hard to determine whether their question was asked because they did not know any better or because they were hoping He would kill Himself. They viewed Jesus as a deceiver, a liar, and a blasphemer.

Knowing what the Jews were thinking and saying to each other, Jesus proceeded to again affirm that He was sent by the Father. They were from "below" and He was from "above," He said. By this He meant they were merely earthlings "of this world." He, by contrast, was from Heaven and "not of this world." In this way, Jesus was again affirming His full equality with God.

These very religious people would die in their sin because they refused to believe that He was all He claimed to be. How do you suppose these people responded to hearing they would never go to heaven as long as they did not believe Jesus was fully God, the Messiah sent from the Father to die for their sins.

Jesus applied the Old Testament divine title "I Am" to Himself. This was one of the major names of God-Jehovah (v. 24 cf. Deuteronomy 32:39). That really riled them. In ridicule they asked Him, "Who are you?" Had He not told them many times before who He was? Yes, He had. It seems they were really thinking, "Who do you think you are?" Quickly, Jesus responded by reminding them who He said He was and verified His claims by His miracles from the first time He met them.

There were many more things Jesus could have said to expose His accusers. He knew them very well, in fact, better than they knew themselves. They must understand that all He had already told them and everything else He could say that would condemn them were things His Father had given Him. If they thought Jesus was too harsh and critical of them, they must realize He spoke only the mind of God.

Without doubt, the Jews knew what Jesus was saying about the Father. They could not miss that. But they were unwilling to agree when He said that He was equal with God and had been sent by Him. These men illustrate that rebellion and rejection produce hardness of heart and hardness of heart produces more hardness. That is a principle that can be seen throughout Scripture. On the other side of that truth there is another principle that prevails through all Scripture. It is that God rewards faith. He welcomes even the smallest faith and gives more faith. To put it another way, He gives more blessing and faith to all who take the first step of faith and acceptance of Him. It is multiplied.

From talking to the Jewish leaders about His heavenly origin and equality with the Father, Jesus broached the subject of His upcoming death by crucifixion. "When you lift up the Son of Man" (v. 28), you will then know that I am who I have been telling you I am. Then you will know I came from the Father and I always do His will.

Notice how Jesus knew who would crucify Him. Here in John 8:28 as in 3:14 and 12:32 when Jesus used the phrase "lift up," it refers to His crucifixion. Here in 8:28 He addressed the Jews accusing Him as the ones who would put Him to death on the cross. We cannot help but wonder what they thought about that. Did they know what He was talking about? Did they think there would ever be a time when they would realize how wrong they had been about Jesus?

Surely, these Jews recognized Jesus' claiming the name of Jehovah for Himself when He said, "Then you will know that I am He" (v. 28). Exodus 3:14 must have come to their minds immediately where God took this name to Himself when He revealed Himself to Moses.

Even through the hours of crucifixion His Father would be with Him. He would not be alone then just as He was not alone when He was here on earth. Then as He would be bearing the sins of the world and as He urged them to accept Him before going to the cross, He only did what pleased the Father (v. 29).

John gives a summary statement about how what Jesus was saying to those who came to ensnare Him was received. We know already that those to whom He was talking directly did not receive Him as their Messiah and Savior. But what about the larger crowd who overheard? "Many came to believe in Him" (v. 30), John said. Was this genuine faith in Him as the Messiah and Savior? It appears so.

The Great I Am as the Son of God, vv. 31–47

Those among the followers of Jesus who believed in Him needed His attention. He gave it to them. They had taken the first step necessary to become part of the family of God. Jesus commended them for that. To be a disciple, a growing maturing child of God, they needed to abide in His Word. This did not mean they needed to work to become God's children or to keep on being His children. What it did mean, and still means today, is those who entered God's family by faith need to be His disciples, or learners, because they are in His family. God's truth recorded in His Word, the Bible, is the means by which we grow in our faith in our walk with God and makes us free from slavery to sin.

Some of those who believed Jesus may only have believed Him in a natural sort of way but not in the sense of placing their eternal destiny in His hands. These were not like the Jews who came to find fault in Him.

Rather, they believed what He said but just had not appropriated it all for themselves, had not personalized it.

It was no doubt these "believers" who expressed denial that they had ever been enslaved (v. 33). They must have forgotten about their ancestors' bondage in Egypt, the captivity in Babylon, and their plight at that time under bondage to Rome. They obviously missed Jesus' point. He was referring to spiritual slavery, slavery to sin (v. 34).

Only Jesus can make someone free from the present bondage and future judgment of sin. You see, these dear people were assuming that simply because they were children of Abraham and since he was never in bondage, neither were they. They evidently thought that physical relationship with Abraham guaranteed spiritual relationship with him. They were wrong in thinking this.

How very inconsistent it was to be a descendant of Abraham and seek to kill Jesus (v. 37). Here He is most assuredly talking to those who had rejected Him. His word, He said, has no place in them. Jesus was obeying His heavenly Father and they claimed to be obeying their earthly father (v. 38). These Jews who were interrogating Jesus laid claim to being children of Abraham. If that is the case, Jesus said then "do the deeds of Abraham" (v. 39). Instead, they were trying hard to kill Jesus. That would not be doing what Abraham would have wanted them to do (v. 40).

It seems the interrogators finally got the point Jesus was making. He was speaking of their spiritual, not physical, ancestry. Who was their spiritual father? They insisted that God was their spiritual father (v. 41). No, Jesus said, He is not your spiritual father. If He had been, they would have loved Jesus instead of hating Him.

These Jews engaged in sarcasm when they said, "We were not born of fornication" (v. 42). What they meant was that Jesus was born of fornication. Rumor had it that Mary conceived out of wedlock. To believe that would, of course, mean the rejection of His virgin birth and everything supernatural about Him.

The Jews may also have meant by the phrase, "We were not born of fornication," that they were not half-breeds like the despised Samaritans among whom He had already ministered (cf. v. 48).

Rather than these people having the only true and living God as their Father, they were told by Jesus that they were of their father the devil (v. 44). Proof of that was that they were busily engaged in doing the devil's desires. The Savior then called Satan a murderer, a liar, and the father of lies (v. 44). No wonder these people did not receive the truth Jesus spoke.

A bold challenge was made by Jesus. A challenge no mere human would ever make seriously. That challenge was, "Which one of you convicts me of sin?" (v. 46). No one in His hearing accepted the challenge. They all knew no fault at all could be found in Him. Since then He spoke the truth, why did they not believe Him? That is what Jesus asked them. And He added, "If you would truly be of God, as you claim, you would believe Me (v. 47).

The Great I Am as the Eternal One, vv. 48–59

In response to Jesus' blunt statement to the Jews (v. 47), they accused Him of siding with the Samaritans (v. 48). The very word Samaritan was a term of contempt and reproach among them. Surely they knew about Jesus' gracious forgiveness of the adulterous Samaritan woman (John 4). You have a demon also, don't you, they said to Jesus. This was their way of trying to get back at Jesus for saying they were not of God and were not even friends of God. The Jews and the Samaritans disagreed on how to worship God and where to worship Him.

Jesus, of course, quickly denied that He was possessed of a demon. "I honor My Father," He said, "and you dishonor me" (v. 49). Then He made another profound statement which made them furious. He promised that those who kept His word would "never see death" (v. 51). That is, they will receive eternal life. Even though all are appointed to die (Hebrews 9:27), those who are rightly related to God will be raised from the dead to live eternally with God.

The Jews with whom Jesus was talking thought He was saying the righteous never die physically. They were convinced beyond doubt therefore that He was possessed of a demon (v. 52). So they reminded Jesus that Abraham and the prophets believed God and they died (v. 53). Why, then, would He say the righteous never die?

Once again, these persistent unbelieving Jews needed to know Jesus was not glorying in Himself but in His heavenly Father. They, on the other hand, gave every evidence that they gloried and boasted in themselves, though they repeatedly claimed the true God was theirs. The Savior told them again they did not know God despite all their claims to the contrary. He even called them liars (v. 55).

What Jesus said next tipped the scale. He called Abraham their father and said Abraham rejoiced to see His day and rejoiced in doing so (v. 56). I can imagine they screamed at Jesus when they said "You are not even fifty years old, and you saw Abraham?" (v. 57). At the time, Jesus was probably thirty-three years old. Interestingly, Jesus had not said He saw Abraham but that Abraham had seen His day. And he had seen it by faith.

Affirming something of great importance was often prefaced with verily, verily or truly, truly. Before Abraham I lived, said Jesus (v. 58). Jesus used the term "I Am" which to the Jews meant He was claiming full deity for Himself (Exodus 6:14). He existed before Abraham was born. He is the eternal Son of God. I hope this key verse will help you think about this portrait of Jesus.

We know the Jews were sure Jesus was claiming to be Jehovah God which they interpreted as blasphemy. And if Jesus is not God, it would have been blasphemy. They, therefore, picked up stones to throw at Him and kill Him. They did not succeed, however, because He escaped from them; His hour had not yet come.

Personal Applications

Was not this a wonderful portrait of Jesus? Are you not thrilled to have Him as your personal Savior and Lord? To forgive our sins, to pay our debt, He had to be God. To be able to die as a Substitute, He had to be man. His is both. He is the God-Man.

This portrait reminds us of all Jesus endured for us. The ridicule and rejection all through His life was unspeakable. But all of that was to demonstrate He was qualified to be the sacrifice for sin.

Throughout His entire life on earth He spoke about His coming death on the cross and His resurrection from the dead. Jesus, the Great I Am, died in the sinner's place. On the cross He was made to be sin for us. He died in our stead. What a Savior!

Study Questions

1. What claims did Jesus make in this portrait?

2. Why did the Jews think Jesus might kill Himself?

3. What did Jesus mean by "lift up the Son of Man"?

4. How did Jesus' teaching about being free and being enslaved go over with the Jews?

5. Did the Jews confronting Jesus come any closer to believing Him in this portrait?

6. Why did the Jews bring up the Samaritans?

7. When you talk to people about Jesus, how do you describe Him?

Giving Sight to a Blind Man

Portrait 13

John 9

"**L**ORD, I believe." This is what the blind man whom Jesus healed said to Him. By this simple and concise affirmation he meant he was accepting Jesus as the Messiah and his Savior. Oh, how wonderful it must have been for him to be able to see for the very first time, physically *and* spiritually.

Before we look at this portrait of Jesus, let's close our eyes tightly and try to walk around in our home or some other safe place. It is hard to keep your eyes closed isn't it? But you can open your eyes when you choose and see again. The man before whom Jesus was standing had never seen the light of day, ever.

All of us take so many things for granted, don't we? It rarely crosses our minds how it would be to try to function without any one of our five senses. How thankful we should be for every blessing from God—the big ones and the small ones.

From the beginning of the Christian era to the present there have always been those whose faith was in Jesus for the here-and-now and for the future. At the same time, there are those whose faith is not in Jesus as their Savior. Unfortunately, unbelief usually produces more unbelief. But thankfully, faith usually grows and matures. We see in this portrait faith growing and unbelief producing more unbelief.

The Wonder of Sight to the Blind Man, vv. 1–7

Not by accident, but with intent, Jesus walked where He knew the blind man would be. We are not told his name. He never saw his parents or anyone else or anything else in his entire life. His world was very, very dark. He was blind from birth. The One who said He was "the light of the world" (John 8:12) in our last portrait of Jesus is about to open this man's blinded eyes.

The twelve disciples were with Jesus at the time. They asked Him who was to blame for the man's blindness. Did he sin or did his parents and is his blindness the judgment of God upon him? Jesus was quick to answer, "It was neither that this man sinned nor his parents" (v. 3). God wants to display His power and love in this man, Jesus said. No sin of the man or his parents was the cause of his blindness. And it was not because God was bringing judgment to him.

Before bringing sight to the man, Jesus reminded His disciples once again that He was the Light of the world. And whenever He is in the world, His function was to be light in the dark world. The light of Jesus and the darkness of sin are striking contrasts.

The blind man, it appears, heard the disciples and Jesus talking about the reason for his plight. Jesus had healed another blind man with only a touch on his eyelids. The disciples and the blind man must have been shocked when Jesus "spat on the ground, and made clay of the spittle, and applied the clay to his eyes" (v. 6).

We are not told why Jesus used this method to remove the man's blindness. It is doubtful that He believed as some of the Jews did that spittle had special healing power. Rather, it seems Jesus wanted to illustrate to the critical Jews who had gathered around Him that the traditions they had added to the law were not equal to the law or even correct. You see, their Sabbath laws stated that it was sin to do what He did on the Sabbath. What Jesus did, therefore, was a challenge to their authority.

Jesus gave sight to the blind man on the Sabbath (v. 14). We find our key verse once again. Furthermore, Jesus could have performed the same miracle without having the man do anything. Did he not heal the man who had not walked for thirty-eight years that way (5:1–5)? Jesus knew that this man who was blind from birth needed to have his faith tested.

At any rate, the man obeyed. That must have been a real challenge for him. The pool to which Jesus told him to go to and wash the mud off his face was some distance from where he was. But he went and did as Jesus told him. With his eyes wide open he came back to where he had been. He could see! Jesus and the twelve may not even have been there when the man returned seeing.

The Witness of the Once-Blind Man, vv. 8–34

Just as it happened after the healing of the man at the pool who had never walked, so it happened here when the blind man was healed by Jesus. Again, this miracle was performed on the Sabbath and the Jews reacted in anger. Before we look at their response to the miracle, let's observe how the man's neighbors responded.

The man who had never seen the light of day must have been well known in the community. Very likely he had to beg for food and other things to survive. Now for the first time ever he sees his neighbors, friends, and family members. Up until now, about all this man could do was sit and beg and be dependent on others for everything.

The neighbors could not agree on what had happened to him. They were all in a state of shock. He did not even look the same. Some said yes this is the man who was blind. Others said no he resembles him, but this person is a different man. All the while, the once-blind man kept insisting to all of them that he in fact was the one-time blind beggar. He was not kidding before and he was not kidding now (v. 9).

"How did your eyes open?" the neighbors wanted to know. He wasted no time to tell them exactly what happened to him. Jesus, He said, made clay and anointed my eyes. Then He told me to go to Siloam and wash. I did just what He told me to do and never questioned anything, the man said. And then he added, "I received sight" (v. 11).

The neighbors wanted to know where this Jesus was. Why? We are not told. Maybe they wanted to question Him. "I do not know," the man said, no doubt with a questioning voice. Surely he too wanted to see this miracle-working Man who gave him sight. To put it mildly, the neighbors were confused over what they witnessed.

The unbelieving Pharisees were the next to visit with the once-blind man. The neighbors took the healed man with them to the Pharisees. There does not seem to have been any pressure on the man. He does not seem to have been forced. The neighbors were not trying to get the man into any trouble. Perhaps the man talked to the neighbors and they decided to go together to the Jewish authorities. After all, it was on the Sabbath when the miracle was performed (v. 14). This must have raised some questions in all of their minds. They must have known about Jesus' claims to be God. "Were the Sabbath laws violated?" they must have wondered.

Instead of getting spiritual help from the Pharisees, they only heard denial of who Jesus was. They did not seem to have denied a miracle had been performed on the man. In fact, to do that would have been stupid of them. The fact that he was blind and now could see could not be denied.

The Pharisees asked the same questions that the neighbors asked. They were given the same answer the neighbors got. The only thing that some of the Pharisees could say was that Jesus was not from God (v. 16), because in their way of thinking He had broken the Sabbath law. Others among the Pharisees asked how a sinner could do such miracles. So there was a great division among the Pharisees over who Jesus was. Then it was that they asked the former blind man who he thought Jesus was. What did they expect to hear from him? His answer was a clever one. He knew about the division among the Pharisees, so he said, "He is a prophet" (v. 18).

Next, the parents of the man born blind, who could now see, were questioned by the Pharisees. Persistent in their stubborn rejection against Jesus, the Pharisees decided to interrogate the beggar's parents (vv. 18–23). "Is this really your son?" they asked the parents. And they added, "who you say was born blind" (v. 19). Admitting that the man could now see, the Pharisees asked how it happened that he received his sight. They really asked the parents three questions: Is he your son? Was he born blind? How can he now see? Surely they knew the answers to each of these questions.

These unbelieving hypocritical antagonists hoped to intimidate them so they would say something they could use against either Jesus or the blind man who now had 20/20 vision. The parents did not seem to hesitate to answer the first two questions. They said, "Yes, he is our boy, and yes he was born blind." To the third question, they waffled. They had not witnessed the miracle and were no doubt very hesitant to say to the Pharisees who they really knew had opened their son's eyes (vv. 20–21).

Surely, these parents would have known by this time that Jesus performed the miracle on their boy. I think, at the very least, they were fudging so they tried to deceive the Pharisees. Maybe you think you would have been braver and stronger in your affirmation of your faith. But remember, the Jewish authorities had already agreed to put out of the synagogue those who confessed faith in Jesus (v. 22). To experience such treatment would put one outside the religious and social community. Such would have to live as lowly outcasts who probably would not be welcomed by Gentiles either.

These parents were not ready to pay that high a price. They said, therefore, "He is of age, ask him" (v. 23). Now what could the Pharisees do? Where could they turn in their diabolic scheme?

This is what they did. For the second time they tried their best to keep the healed man from giving Jesus the credit for his sight. Jesus is a sinner, they said, admit it. This was nothing short of seeking to create a contrast between Jesus and God. This despite the fact that Jesus claimed to be equal with God and was sent by Him to the earth and proved by His miracle-working power that His claims were true. So these men admitted that God had healed the man but that Jesus had nothing to do with it.

Believe and/or accuse whatever and whomever you want was the essence of the once-blind man's response. One thing I do know, "I was blind and now I see" (v. 25). What the healed said then must have really irritated Jesus' critics. When they asked again the same questions he had already answered before, the man said to them, Are you thinking about being His disciples also? That, of course was the very last thing they had planned to do or even to think about doing. Today we would say that to ask such a question was the last straw.

Their response to what he said made them angry. They "reviled" (v. 28) Him and in essence said you be His disciple, we would much rather be Moses' disciples (v. 28). They even claimed not to know where Jesus even came from. But Moses was their man. God spoke to him, not to Jesus.

For having been blind all his life, the man showed keen insight into the hardened hearts of his accusers. He proceeded to preach a short sermon to them (vv. 30–34). He used the Pharisees' own axiom against them— God does not hear sinners. Since Jesus could heal him by appealing to God and God answered by healing him, He could not be a sinner. No one else who had been blind from birth had ever been made to see until Jesus met this man and performed a miracle. The man pressed the Pharisees further as he exhorted them: "If this man were not from God, He could do nothing" (v. 33).

Finally, the faithless Pharisees accused the once-blind man of being born in sin and they had heard all they wanted to hear from him. So they put him out of the synagogue. Remember, this was what his parents were afraid of and escaped because they refused to tell how their son was made to see.

The Worship of the Once-Blind Man, vv. 35–41

Word spread about the one-time beggar who would need to beg no more being put out of the synagogue. Why? Because he refused to disbelieve Jesus was a sinner and had not been sent by God. The Pharisees demanded of him to be like they were, unbridled unbelievers.

Jesus heard that he was thrown out of the synagogue and looked him up. He found him asked him a totally different question than the Pharisees had asked, "Do you believe in the Son of Man?" He asked him (v. 35). With child-like faith he said, "And who is He, Lord, that I may believe in Him?" (v. 36).

With that response from the man, Jesus introduced Himself to him. He prefaced His answer with a reference to his sight, reminding him he was looking and talking to the Son of Man. Quickly, the man said, "I believe." And that is not all he did. He also worshipped Jesus.

This act of the once-blind man should remind us that we too are to worship Jesus in response to His acceptance of us in His family. Before we trusted Jesus as our Sin-bearer, we were spiritually blind, without God and without hope. Worship is a welcome response to faith.

It was in the public place where Jesus and the once-blind man met. It was not a private meeting. Others gathered around them and heard what the two said to each other. Among those who gathered were the Pharisees. Jesus turned and faced these hypocrites eyeball to eyeball.

First, He told them one of His purposes in coming into the world was to bring judgment (v. 39). Those who are blind either physically or spiritually or both would be made to see. And also those who have physical sight but are spiritually blind would become even more blinded and hardened because of their persistent unbelief (v. 39).

What Jesus said bothered the Pharisees greatly, and they asked Him a final question. They asked, "We are not blind too, are we?" (v. 40). They all had their physical eyesight so they were not asking about that. Rather, they wanted to know if they were said to be spiritually blind. It seems they were hoping for a negative answer, but they did not get it. Jesus made it very clear that because they refused again and again to accept Him for who He claimed to be, they were spiritually blind. They could see with their physical eyes but were blind spiritually.

Personal Applications

This portrait shows extremes of both faith and unbelief and the progression of both. The blind man who had his sight restored developed in his faith as he learned more about Jesus. The Jews who dogged His every move became more and more determined not to believe. We should learn from this how important faith is and how damaging unbelief is.

There is a lesson for all of us in the way the parents of the once-blind man behaved. They feared being shut off from everything they valued and so they simply would not answer the third question the Pharisees asked them. Instead they sent them to their son. The application for us is, How often do we stop short of putting the claims of Christ before those who need Him so badly? Hopefully we will be bold from now on like the healed man and not be ashamed to claim Jesus as our Lord and Savior.

Study Questions

1. Why do you think Jesus did not give the man sight by just opening his eyes without putting clay on his eyes and then telling him to go and wash it off?

2. Are there any physical maladies which are the result of sin? If so, name some.

3. What do the different responses to the miracle in this portrait tell us?

4. Why did the Pharisees become increasingly hardened in this portrait of Jesus?

5. Which comes first, faith or worship? Why?

6. Do you know any people who are still blind to what Jesus wants to do for them?

7. How are you going to reach them? When do you plan to try?

Divine Shepherd

Portrait 14

John 10

I<small>N OUR</small> last portrait of Jesus He gave sight to a man who was born blind. The Savior applied wet clay to the man's eyes and sent him to the pool of Siloam to wash it off. The blind man did as Jesus told him. When the clay was washed off, he could see for the first time in his life.

Jesus performed the miracle on the Jewish Sabbath and that caused the Pharisees to think they had caught Jesus breaking the Sabbath law. He silenced them and told them they were spiritually blind and would remain in that condition until they would accept Him for all He claimed to be—very God of very God.

The portrait of Jesus as the divine Shepherd and His people as sheep is in striking contrast to the last portrait of Him giving sight to a blind man. The word sheep describes Jesus' people collectively. The plural of this word is always used. Eighteen times in this passage Jesus is described as a Shepherd. The Jews to whom He spoke knew very well the role of shepherds with their sheep.

Imagine seeing a single shepherd out on the Judean hills. He is wearing a turban on his head and the customary long robe-like garment. In his hand is the shepherd's crook, a cane-like object, which he is moving across the brush and short grass to be sure there is nothing there that would injure the sheep. They are behind him grazing and moving slowly as he moves on for more grazing. He never drives them but always leads them, looking back, checking them periodically to be sure they are safe. Oh, do you see that one small sheep over there caught in a thicket? He is struggling to get loose and is about to fall over the edge of the rocky cliff. With haste, there goes the shepherd. He gets as close to the edge as he can without falling over it himself. Now he is reaching out and down with his long crook. He puts it under the sheep's neck and gently pulls it up to safety.

Now try to put yourself in the place of that sheep that needed the help of the shepherd. If you are one of God's sheep, your Shepherd is Jesus, God's Son. We too often, like sheep, wander away from our Shepherd. We get caught in thickets of sin and need our Shepherd's caring, loving help. We all need Him to go before us. We all need to follow Him. He is our divine Shepherd.

Let us gaze upon this portrait of Jesus which John has painted for us. He has included in his portrait five different characteristics or perfections of Jesus the divine Shepherd. He is the true Shepherd, the good Shepherd, the sacrificial Shepherd, the obedient Shepherd, and the faithful Shepherd.

Jesus, the True Shepherd, vv. 1–6

The oriental sheepfold was and still is very different from what we might think of when we hear the word. It was where the shepherds brought their sheep in the evening. The enclosure was a rather large area surrounded with rock and brushes and of course without a roof. There was one opening where the sheep from a number of shepherds would enter. After all the sheep were in the sheepfold, someone acted as a gatekeeper, or doorkeeper, so the sheep could not get out and no one could get in. This task was performed by one of the shepherds or one learning to become a shepherd.

Shepherds returned in the morning to claim their sheep and take them out to pasture. The sheep knew the voice of their shepherd. He called them by name and one by one they came to the opening and followed their shepherd. The sheep would not follow a stranger. Instead, they would flee from them.

Thieves and robbers would often crawl over the walls and steal the sheep. These might be called rustlers. There were two kinds. Thieves would steal after much planning and forethought. Robbers, on the other hand, usually used violence to accomplish their wicked goal.

John called what Jesus had just told the Pharisees a "figure of speech" or a parable. He also tells us Israel's religious leaders did not understand what those things were which He had been saying to them (v. 6). They did not understand that Jesus was telling them that all the false messiahs who came before Him and even the Pharisees who rejected Him as the true Messiah sent from God were like the thieves and robbers who attacked the sheep. He was trying to tell them plainly that He was the only true Shepherd.

Jesus, the Good Shepherd, vv. 7–11

Again, Jesus used the "truly, truly" which was to emphasize the great importance of what followed (v. 7 cf. v. 1). The expression is common in John's Gospel. Once again, Jesus sought to make clear to all that He was the only Way into God's family; He was the Door of the sheepfold (v. 7). All others who came before Him He called thieves and robbers. The true prophets of God were not included in this statement but only those who made false claims. Believing Israelites did believe the true prophets and the angel from heaven who all predicted that Jesus the true Messiah would come and deliver His people from their sin (Isaiah 9:6; Micah 5:2; Luke 1:31; 2:21).

Jesus said He came to earth to give eternal life to all who accepted Him as God's Son and Savior. He is not only the true Shepherd as opposed to all the false ones. He is also the good Shepherd (in contrast to the bad ones, the false ones) "who gave His life, who died in the place of sinners (v. 11). Memorize this verse. It is key to remembering this portrait of Jesus. Only Jesus is the Way of access to God the Father for salvation and spiritual nourishment (v. 9).

Jesus, the Sacrificial Shepherd, vv. 12–17

Long before Jesus was born of the Virgin Mary, God had ordained and appointed the office of priests within the tribe of Levy to be His people's spiritual leaders and teachers. The Pharisees who persisted in opposing Jesus were not ordained by God and arose between Old Testament times and New Testament times.

The priests of old were set apart as God's guardians of His people until the true, good, and sacrificial Shepherd would come. Jesus came and was seeking to identify Himself as that Shepherd. He was not a "hired hand" (v. 12) but was the Shepherd. The "hired hand" is not the same as the thief, the robber, or the wolf. But since the hired hand does not own the sheep, he sometimes forsakes them in time of danger. He has his own interests at heart rather than those of the sheep.

Jesus clearly contrasts Himself with the hired hand. "Jesus is the good Shepherd." He knows His own and they know Him (v. 14). God the Father knows Jesus His Son and Jesus knows God. They are both of the same divine essence. They are one in essence (9:30). As the sacrificial Shepherd Jesus said, "I lay down my life for the sheep" (10:15). He died in our place, in our stead.

The "other sheep" (v. 16) Jesus refers to are most likely Gentiles. He did not come to give His life only for Jews, His own people. Gentiles, Greeks, Samaritans, all non-Jews were also those for whom He died as their Substitute. He is the Shepherd of all who receive Him as their personal Savior.

To lay down one's life for others is one thing. It is, to be sure, a noble and loving thing to do. But to be able to take it up again, to be resurrected, is quite another. Jesus in this beautiful portrait did both. He died in our place and He raised Himself up again (v. 17). God the Father and the Holy Spirit were also involved in His resurrection, but here Jesus is clearly stating His own part.

Jesus, the Obedient Shepherd, vv. 17–18

Our Lord's resurrection from the dead is proof of His absolute sovereignty over death, hell and Satan. What a wonderful Shepherd God's sheep have. Are you one of His sheep?

No one took Jesus' life. The Romans did not and neither did the unbelieving rebellious Jews. He gave His life voluntarily and He raised it up again. One who has conquered death can do anything. Jesus was indeed obedient unto death, even death on a cross, the most despicable form of death (Philippians 2:8). He "by the grace of God" tasted "death for everyone" (Hebrews 2:9). He could have called upon His Father for holy angels to come and rescue Him but He did not (Matthew 26:53).

Jesus, the Faithful Shepherd, vv. 19–29

As happened so many times before, there arose a division among the Jews because of what Jesus said. In some instances the division was even among the Pharisees. They did not all agree on everything. Among the Jewish people at large there was even more division because of Jesus. There simply was not a consensus among them over how they viewed Jesus.

In this instance, as was true before, some said Jesus had a demon meaning He was possessed of a demon. He was viewed as insane. Those who viewed Him this way could not even understand why those who did not agree with them would even listen to Him. But others could not forget how this same Jesus had opened the eyes of the man who was blind from birth (9:13–18). They insisted that someone who can make a person see who had never seen anything from his birth could not have a demon (vv. 19–21).

Confusion arose among the Jews over what Jesus had taught about His identifying Himself as the divine Shepherd. It seems rather unsuspected since He used something which was very familiar to them—sheep and shepherds. He spoke very plainly to them. No doubt, the spiritual darkness that surrounded many of them kept them from understanding what He taught.

The division among them which we discussed above was followed by serious doubt about His claims.

It seems whenever Jesus was in Jerusalem, He taught in the courts of the temple. There the people gathered to hear Him and often to question Him. From the beginning of His public ministry He referred to the temple as His Father's house (2:16; 5:43; 7:28; 8:2, 20). This time it was the time of the Feast of Dedication. It is believed to have taken place in the middle of December. This is the only reference to the Feast in the Bible. History records that one Judas Maccabaeus began the celebration about 165 B.C. It was to remember how the temple was dedicated after it had been desecrated by Antiochus Epiphanes. In Jewish religion today this Feast is known by its Hebrew name, Hanukkah.

The question the Jews asked Jesus was, "How long will you keep us in suspense? If you are the Christ, tell us plainly" (v. 24). I do not know how much plainer He could tell them who He was. It was not that He had not told them before. Rather, it was they had been so blinded that they did not believe. Hardness of their hearts produced more hardness. Jesus had not only told them who He was. His works also verified that what He claimed was true. These who asked the question were not His sheep. They were not His sheep because they refused to believe and trust Him.

Jesus told them again those who believe in Me are My sheep and they follow Me (v. 27). He then told these who had not believed Him that those who do believe have eternal life. He gives to those who believe eternal life and that is not all—they will never perish. No one would ever snatch them out of His hand. It is not our holding on to His hand but His holding on to ours that secures us. He will never lose His grip on us. What a blessed truth that is. Jesus' sheep have been given to Him by His heavenly Father. Since He is greater than all, no one is able to take His own out of His hand. So it is not only that Jesus' sheep are in His hand but they are also in His Father's hand (vv. 28–29). There is no greater security and protection than this.

Think back when you were held by the hand of your parent or when you held on to your parent's hand. When you stumbled while holding your parent's hand, you fell. But when your parent held your hand and you stumbled, their hand kept you from falling. As God's child, your hand is held by God, and He will never let you go.

Jesus, the Divine Shepherd, vv. 30–38

We have here in verse 30 one of the strongest affirmations of Jesus' absolute deity. He said, "I and the Father are one." They are each separate Persons but they share equally of the same divine essence. This statement from Jesus plus the one before it where He once again called God "My Father' (v. 29) caused the Jews to again try to kill Him by stoning Him (v. 31).

How did Jesus respond this time? First, He asked them for which of His good works performed before their very eyes they wanted to stone Him. It was not because of any of His good works but because He had by both of the above statements made Himself equal with God (v. 33). Second, He then appealed to Psalm 82:6 where the psalmist under the Spirit's guidance called the judges in Israel "gods" recognizing their authority to carry out justice. Jesus' point was, "You Jewish leaders do not charge the psalmist of blasphemy so why do you say I have blasphemed because I said I am the Son of God ?" (vv. 34–35).

Further, Jesus challenged His opponents. Even though the Jewish leaders before Him did not believe the miracles He performed were works of the Father through Him He begged them to believe that the works He did were works of God even if they did not believe Him. This made them even more angry and determined to silence Him. They tried to seize Him but He "eluded their grasp" (v. 39).

Jesus then went back to where His forerunner, John the Baptist, was baptizing. Many people flocked around Him there and a goodly number believed in Him. The folks there said that everything John the Baptist said about Jesus was true.

Personal Applications

What a wonderful Shepherd is Jesus our Lord. The question is, Are we allowing Him to lead us? Are we following Him? How do we do that? We do it by obeying His Word to us. This involves not only believing the Bible to be all it claims to be but obeying its teaching for us also. It means living according to Scripture.

The songwriter put it very well when he said, "Turn your eyes upon Jesus. Look full in His wonderful face and the things of earth will grow strangely dim in the light of His glory and grace." We learn to know Jesus the incarnate Word, the personal Word of God, as we learn from the written Word of God, the Bible.

The next time you face an important decision, seek the guidance from Jesus the divine Shepherd. He has promised to be with us always and to give us peace that passes all understanding. He will walk with His people through troubled waters. He will be there when it seems that everyone else has forsaken you.

Study Questions

1. Can you name the various descriptions from this portrait of Jesus as the divine Shepherd?

2. Why do you think Jesus chose to liken Himself to a shepherd?

3. Why do you think Jesus chose to liken His people to sheep?

4. What did Jesus say in this portrait that affirmed His full and absolute deity?

5. Do you think you could be used of God to be one of Jesus' undershepherds? He wants us to feed His lambs.

Resurrection and the Life

Portrait 15

John 11

JESUS HAS power over life and death. He proved this when He raised Lazarus from the dead. As believers in Jesus as our sin-bearer, we have hope beyond the grave. The resurrection of Jesus Himself which we will see in a portrait of Him later and His raising of Lazarus provide great hope for our own resurrection.

In the portrait we are looking at now Jesus said to Martha, sister of Lazarus, "I am the resurrection and the life; he who believes in Me shall live even if he dies" (v. 25).

It is hard to imagine how hard the hearts of Jesus' enemies really were. They completely rejected all His claims to have God as His Father and all His miracles to demonstrate the truthfulness of those claims. They are going to do the same again even though He raises Lazarus from the dead. Hardness of heart and unbelief really do produce more hardness and more unbelief, does it not?

As we take a long and careful look at this portrait of Jesus, watch for His sovereign love and care for the dying and the grieving. And do not miss seeing the rebellious, bitter hatred for Jesus by the religious leaders of His day.

The more we examine this portrait of Jesus, the clearer several different attitudes toward death become. And, of course, once again, the attitude of the Jews toward Jesus looms large in this portrait. The longer they were around Him and the more they saw Him do and say, the more animosity they had toward Him.

Before we look too intently at this portrait of Jesus, let us listen to what some youngsters had to say about dying and death. In a *Good Housekeeping* magazine the following appeared: Alan, age 7: "God doesn't tell you when you are going to die because He wants it to be a big surprise." Aaron, age 8: "The hospital is the place where people go on their way to

93

heaven." Raymond, age 10: "A good doctor can help you so you won't die. A bad doctor sends you to heaven." Stephanie, age 9: "Doctors help you so you won't die until you pay all their bills." Marsha, age 9: "When you die, you don't have to do homework in heaven unless your teacher is there too." Kevin, age 10: "I'm not afraid to die because I'm a Boy Scout." Ralph, age 8: "When birds are ready to die, they just fly to heaven."

Now fix your eyes on Jesus as the Resurrection and the Life. He, with power to turn water into wine, give sight to the blind, and cause those who never walked before to walk, is going to delay going to see and heal His friend who lies close to death and, in fact, dies before He gets there. Why?

Jesus Allows His Friend to Die, vv. 1–16

His very special friend's name was Lazarus. He lived with his two sisters, Mary and Martha, who were also Jesus' special friends. They lived in the little village of Bethany. Lazarus was deathly ill. Mary and Martha sent someone to tell Jesus about his condition. At the time Jesus and His disciples were in a place called Perea just across the Jordan River from Bethany. "The one you love is sick," they told Jesus.

When He got the news, He said to the one who was sent to tell Him and to the disciples, "This sickness is not unto death, but for the glory of God, that the Son of God may be glorified by it" (v. 4). Jesus did not mean by this that Lazarus would not ever die but that his death would not be permanent–he would be brought back to life again. A bit later Jesus told the disciples that He would wake Lazarus from his "sleep" of death (v. 11).

That which was a very sad thing for Mary and Martha to accept was going to turn out to bring glory or praise to both God the Father and God the Son.

Instead of going immediately to be with Lazarus and his sisters, Jesus stayed where He was two more days. That seemed very strange to the disciples and even more disconcerting to Mary and Martha. Did Jesus need to be there to attend to Lazarus' needs—to heal him? No, He did not. After all, He healed a nobleman's son from a distance (4:46). Surely Lazarus' illness was no more difficult to overcome than the blindness of the man who had never seen anything (9:1, 11).

After the two-day delay Jesus said to the disciples, "Let us go to Judea again" (v. 7). Bethany was in Judea. That request scared the disciples. They reminded Jesus, as though He had forgotten, that it was in Judea where the

Jews were recently trying to stone Him. Jesus assured His fearful disciples as long as He was living in accordance with His Father's will, all would be well.

There must be no misunderstanding on the part of the disciples. Lazarus was not asleep physically. Jesus used the term "sleep" as a euphemism of death. Lazarus is dead, Jesus told them. And He was glad that he was so that the disciples could witness His resurrection power.

Doubting Thomas, as he is often called, had a word for his fellow fearful disciples. "Let us go and die with him" (v. 16), he said. Given the expressed fear of the disciples, it seems that Thomas meant that the disciples should stay loyal to Jesus to the very end. He must have felt certain that the Jews would kill Jesus when they found Him there and he did not want to forsake Jesus but rather wanted to die with Him.

Jesus Comforts the Sorrowing, vv. 17–37

When Jesus and the disciples arrived at the home of Mary and Martha, Lazarus had been in the tomb four days. Friends had gathered to comfort and give their condolences to the sisters. Since Bethany was only about two miles away from Jerusalem, many Jews who were friends of Mary and Martha even came to show their concern.

Martha, the more aggressive of the sisters, found out Jesus was arriving and she went to meet Him. Mary stayed at home and waited. When Martha approached Jesus, she immediately mildly scolded Him. "If you had been here, my brother would not have died" (v. 21), she said. What she said implied that Lazarus died because Jesus was late getting there. Did she not know He could have healed her brother from a distance if He had wanted to? Martha's statement put emphasis upon herself. The order of the pronoun "my" reveals she very much resented that she too was affected by Jesus' delay.

Jesus assured Martha that her brother would rise again because He was the Resurrection and the Life (v. 25). This verse is the key that helps us remember the portrait.. She thought He was talking about the future resurrection of all believers. Jesus reminded her that He not only had power to raise the dead in the future but could do that now for her brother. "Do you believe that whoever lives and believes in me shall live forever?" Jesus asked her. Martha's response made clear that she did believe Jesus was the Messiah, the Son of God, but she was not at all sure He could bring her brother back to life (vv. 26–27).

Martha went then and told Mary that Jesus wanted to see her. Quickly, Mary stopped what she was doing and went to see Jesus. He was not even in town yet when she met Him. Those who were trying to comfort Mary thought she was going to Lazarus' grave to weep there.

As soon as Mary saw Jesus, she hurried to Him, fell at His feet and worshipped Him. While she was at His feet, she said something similar yet different from what Martha said to Jesus. The wording in the English is the same. But the sentence structure in the original Greek is different. The order in which she put her words put emphasis not upon herself as Martha had done, but upon her brother. This reveals she was not giving attention to herself as Martha had. She was more concerned with her brother than with Mary.

Mary cried, the Jews with her cried, Jesus saw them crying and He cried. Together they all, except Jesus, assumed Lazarus would not be with them any longer. Jesus knew that in a few minutes He would bring Lazarus back to life. When the friendly Jews who were close to Mary and Martha saw Jesus in tears, some of them said to each other, "Behold, how He loved him" (v. 36). Others among them raised the question of why He did not keep Lazarus from dying (v. 37). This appears to be a subtle inference that Jesus' tears may not have been genuine. The answer to their question was, Yes, Jesus certainly could have healed him. However, allowing him to die and then raising Him from the dead would bring more glory to God the Father and to Jesus, and that is what He was seeking. And it should also always be what we seek.

Jesus Raises the Dead, vv. 38–44

With great sincerity and sorrow Jesus was emotionally moved over Lazarus' death and how it affected Lazarus' sisters. He was not play-acting here, He was "deeply moved within." He went to the tomb where Lazarus' body had been placed. It was a typical burial site in that day and time.

Martha who was probably not expecting Jesus to bring her brother back to life was told to remove the stone in front of the tomb. Under ordinary circumstances the way she responded to Jesus' request was normal. Not having been embalmed as the dead are today, there would have been a foul odor after four days. But these were not ordinary circumstances. Jesus reminded Martha of what He had told her earlier—God would be glorified through her brother's death.

Those who followed Jesus to the burial site rolled the stone away (v. 41), and He gave thanks to His Father in prayer. As we see Him praying, we can also hear Him telling the Father that He knows He is being heard by Him. When the prayer was concluded Jesus called out loudly, "Lazarus, come forth," "This way out." Since Lazarus was bound and had the burial cloth over his face, he needed to follow the sound of Jesus' voice (v. 43). As soon as Lazarus got out of the grave, Jesus told those watching to "unbind him, and let him go" (v. 44). And they did as they were told. Imagine how they must have felt as they took off the bands of cloth from his body. He was alive again.

Jesus Pursued to be Put to Death, vv. 45–57

We do not know how many Jews had come to be with Mary, but some of them believed in Jesus when they saw Lazarus come out of the grave. Others of them went to the Pharisees and reported what they had heard and seen. Why did they go to them? We are not told why but some of them without any evil intent may have wanted to simply report what Jesus had done. Perhaps they would change their attitude toward Jesus.

The result of their visit and report was that there was a council convened by the Pharisees to consider what they should do about Jesus and how they should respond to His performing of miracles. The Pharisees had to face up to the fact that Jesus was performing many signs or miracles (v. 47). If they did nothing, they were afraid more and more people would believe in Him. If that happened, the Roman authorities would no longer allow the Jews to conduct religious services and that would essentially mean the end of the nation (v. 48).

One named Caiaphas, the high priest that year, interrupted the discussion about what to do with Jesus. He came up with a political plan which turned out to be a prophecy which came to pass though he certainly did not intend that. In brief, his plan was to proceed with the capture and killing of Jesus because that would be better than to have the Romans put an end to the Jewish nation, that is, to remove all religious freedom from them. Caiaphas and others feared Jesus would become so popular that He and His followers would agitate the Romans to the point that they all would incur Rome's wrath upon them. This was, simply put, a politically expedient scheme devised by those who hated Jesus.

It is indeed true. Jesus did die for the nation of Israel and for all mankind though Caiaphas had no sympathy for or interest in that truth. The suggestion of Caiaphas apparently was overwhelmingly received by his peers. From that time on, they agreed on the plan and pursued Jesus aggressively.

Jesus knew of the diabolic plan of the Sanhedrin and traveled to Ephraim. This town was about twenty miles north of Jerusalem near a wilderness.

The Passover celebration was about to take place. Some thought Jesus would show up for it in Jerusalem. No one could find Him though some searched diligently for Him. The authorities even issued orders that it was to be reported to them if anyone knew where He was (v. 57).

No one found Him. It was not yet the hour appointed by the Father that He should die for the sins of mankind.

Personal Applications

Jesus allowed His friend Lazarus to die so that He could raise him from the dead. He wanted to give those who were rejecting Him another opportunity to believe in Him.

We often do not know why trials and bad things happen to us and those we love. Jesus wants us to trust Him even when we cannot understand why. He wanted the same from Mary and Martha when their brother died. Their faith needed to be strengthened. Jesus knew that more than they did.

We often do as Martha did—indirectly blame Jesus for not doing something when we wanted it done. Always, we must remember He has the best time and our best interests in mind as He relates to us.

Jesus was so divine He could raise the dead and so human He cried. He sorrowed when His good friend died. He knows all about us too. He is still touched with the feelings of our infirmities. His way is always best for us in all the circumstances of life.

No matter how much His opponents rejected Him and tried to kill Him, Jesus kept on giving them His Word and performing miracles before their very eyes. We too need to take heart when we fail to get the results we expect as we serve Him. He rewards faithfulness and obedience to Him.

Study Questions

1. Why do you think Jesus allowed His friend to die?

2. Did the disciples have genuine cause to fear when Jesus decided to go near Jerusalem?

3. What was different about Martha's response and Mary's response to Jesus when He came to their house?

4. What did Jesus do before He raised Lazarus from the dead?

5. Why did the Jews agree to pursue Jesus to death?

6. Have you been encouraged in your view of death by the study of this portrait of Jesus?

7. How has your faith been strengthened?

King without a Throne

Portrait 16

John 12:1–19

IN THIS portrait of Jesus, He begins the last week of His life before His crucifixion. In the next portrait of Him, He is anticipating the cross. The remaining nine chapters in John are each devoted to Jesus' death. That means the first eleven chapters are devoted to His birth and ministry with His disciples.

Through this portrait of Jesus we will see Him observe the last Passover. We will also watch as He is entertained in the home of Mary, Martha, and Lazarus in Bethany. We should remember that it was in this town with these friends that He raised Lazarus from the dead.

In addition, let us watch how Mary's reception of Jesus is welcomed in contrast to Judas Iscariot's rejection. Observe also how the townsfolk welcomed Jesus as He made His triumphal entry into the city of Jerusalem. Then it was they hailed Him as the King of Israel. This was a joyous occasion except for Judas and the Pharisees. The latter were terribly upset because many were becoming Jesus' followers and that would not bode well for them.

Notice the three very different responses to Jesus in this portrait.

Personal Devotion of Jesus, vv. 1–11

It would have been very dangerous for Jesus to stay over in Jerusalem when He needed lodging or respite. Besides, He would not have been able to afford extravagant facilities. Instead, He often made His home with friends in Bethany. The authorities had already made a compact to kill Him. Six days before Passover, Jesus and His disciples arrived at the home of Mary, Martha, and their brother Lazarus, His once-dead friend.

A supper was prepared for Jesus and those with Him. Martha, true to her character, was serving the food. Lazarus was also there. It seems he had gone away from Bethany for awhile after he was brought back to life. Maybe this was true because he feared the Pharisees would seek to kill him too. John does seem to go out of his way to mention the presence of Lazarus who was reclining at the table with Jesus (v. 2).

Mary was there also. And she was doing what she delighted in doing, worshipping Jesus. This she did by spending what must have been her savings for a long time to buy costly perfume. With this, she anointed His feet and wiped them with her hair. When she did that, and when Judas Iscariot either smelled the fragrance throughout the house or saw her do it, Judas complained.

He said with a rebuke, "Why was this perfume not sold and the money given to feed the poor?" In other words, he viewed what Mary did as an extravagant waste. The "three hundred denarii," he said, could have been gotten for it, would have been almost the annual wages for a an unprofessional worker.

John tells us Judas Iscariot was not saying this because he was concerned for the poor but because he was a thief. The others knew this because he was like the treasurer of the group and was known to take some of the money for himself (v. 6). Jesus was quick to respond to Judas who had already determined to betray Jesus to His enemies. "Let her alone," Jesus said, "in order that she may keep it for the day of My burial" (v. 7). He further reminded Judas and all in the hearing of His voice that the poor would always be present but He would not be.

It would be fair to say that Mary had a deeper understanding of what lay ahead for Jesus than His disciples exhibited. He had told these men a number of times before that He would die and be raised from the dead. But they never seemed to get it or its results. His death should not have been a secret to them.

Early on in the portrait of Jesus as the Savior of Sinners (chap. 3) He said He would be lifted up just as Moses lifted up the serpent in the wilderness (3:14). In the Living Bread portrait He said the bread He would give for the life of the world was His flesh (6:51). The Jews were constantly seeking to kill Him (7:19). Jesus told the Jews, "When you lift up the Son of Man, then you will know that I am He" (8:28). As the Divine Shepherd, Jesus said He would lay down His life so He could take it again or raise it up (10:17). The disciples also knew the enemies of Jesus had already called for His arrest and death (11:57). Mary took all of these statements very seriously. That is why she gave the gift of expensive ointment to display her love for and faith in Jesus.

The resurrection of Lazarus caused quite a stir in and around the little village of Bethany, and well it should have. As soon as word got out that Jesus was at Mary and Martha's home, a large crowd came. No doubt, many of them were from the Galilee area. They had heard about Jesus there and very likely saw Him and His miracles. So they came to see Him again and to witness more of His work. But John makes sure we understand they also came to see Lazarus—the once-dead man who was now alive and well (v. 9). After all, they had never before seen a dead person brought back to life.

Some of the chief priests were also there but with a totally different agenda. They had decided to take Lazarus and put him to death. As far as they were concerned, he was having too many people following him. The miracle Jesus performed on him caused many to believe on Jesus (vv. 10–11).

Public Acclaim of Jesus, vv. 12–19

The next day, Sunday before the Passover, after the meal at Mary, Martha, and Lazarus' home in Bethany, another large crowd who had come for the Passover celebration serenaded Jesus as He rode into the city of Jerusalem. They gathered branches from the palm trees to wave as He went by on a colt. Luke, in his account, tells us how Jesus sent two disciples ahead to arrange for the donkey or colt. He also describes how the people not only waved palm branches but also spread garments on the roadway (Luke 19:28–36). In addition to all of this they cried out, "Hosanna! Blessed is He who comes in the name of the Lord, even the King of Israel" (John 12:13). Here they were reciting Psalm 118:25–26. "Hosanna" means "save now I pray you."

These common people were no doubt thinking of being delivered from Roman oppression as they quoted these verses. Even their rabbis viewed these verses as Messianic in nature. The people knew Psalm 118 very well. They often sang it at Passover and other special days. Some think Jesus and His disciples may even have sung it together at the Last Supper (Matthew 26:30).

Imagine how enraged the Pharisees and chief priests must have been to hear this. What could they do? The people were hailing Jesus as the King of Israel, just as they feared would happen. What did the Roman authorities think of this? They also must have thought they were about to have a rebellion on their hands.

In fulfillment of prophecy John tells us Jesus sat on the donkey. He then quotes Zechariah 9:9: "Fear not daughter of Zion; behold, your King is coming, seated on a donkey's colt" (v. 15). Hundreds of years before Jesus was born, the prophet called Him Israel's King. That makes verse 15 key.

The disciples did not understand what it all meant. They were puzzled and confused. Later, they did begin to put all the pieces of the puzzle together. Only after Jesus was raised from the dead and glorified, did they understand. What they did not understand at first was how in Jesus the Old Testament Scriptures were being fulfilled before their very eyes. The persistent attempts to kill Him and even His forerunner, John the Baptist, all began to make sense in fulfillment of Scripture.

The language used to describe the crowds of people who came to see Jesus and Lazarus implies a very large number. No wonder the Pharisees were all worked up. They were losing popularity, and Jesus seemed to be gaining it.

Frustration and Fear of the Pharisees, v. 19

It was expected. They were at wits end, you might say. Here it is, just before the Passover Feast and a large crowd gathers in Bethany to see Jesus and hear Him. He was viewed by them as the miracle-worker. Then in the city of Jerusalem He is hailed as the One who fulfilled the Psalmist's portrayal.

As so often happens when the opposition can not be silenced, the accusers turn on each other in frustration and anger. These bewildered Pharisees in our portrait of Jesus as King without a Throne turn on each other. They said to one another, "You see that you are not doing any good; look, the world has gone after Him" (v. 19). That was a bit of exaggeration, but they certainly were losing their grip on the people. The real issue was they feared losing their authority. We might say that they found themselves between the rock and the hard place.

Personal Applications

This portrait of Jesus reminds us that we should give generously to Jesus and His work here and now. We need to learn how to sacrifice for our Lord as Mary did. Worship of our Savior and Lord is so essential. Time spent in His presence is not wasted. It is absolutely essential.

God would have each of His children become more like Jesus every day. We love when He showers blessings on us but are we eager to become more like Him? God is grieved when we become dulled and insensitive to Him and His work. Too, we must not forget that when people reject Jesus, whether it be for salvation or His lordship in their lives, God the Father has been rejected also.

Study Questions

1. Why did Jesus spend so much time in Bethany?

2. How would you contrast Judas and Mary?

3. How would you contrast Judas and Martha?

4. Why did the chief priests plan to kill Lazarus? What did he do wrong?

5. What can you do starting today to show to Jesus your love and devotion to Him?

6. Do you think all the people in the two crowds had trusted Jesus as their Savior?

Anticipating the Cross

Portrait 17

John 12:20–50

THE REALITY of His death on a cross was not something which dawned upon Jesus after He learned how determined the Jewish authorities were to kill Him. No, He became one of us so that He might die for our sins. All of us were born dying. That is, as soon as life begins, death begins also. Jesus, however, was not born dying. He was born so that He could die.

Isaiah the prophet of old predicted Jesus' coming to this world. He described Him as ". . . despised and forsaken of men, a man of sorrows, and acquainted with grief. . . . But He was pierced through for our transgressions, He was crushed for our iniquities" (Isaiah 53:3, 5).

In the last portrait we saw Jesus being acclaimed by the crowd as "king of Israel" (John 12:13). His triumphal entry into the city of Jerusalem caused the Pharisees to panic because they said, "The whole world has gone after Him" (v. 19).

Some Greeks were among those who had come for the Passover Feast. These searched out the disciples and made it known to them that they wanted to see Jesus. Their visit and request prompted Jesus to say, "The hour has come for the Son of Man to be glorified" (v. 23). We will see Him in this portrait which John paints as Anticipating the Cross.

Greeks Seek Jesus, vv. 20–22

John does not tell us who these people were except that they were Greeks. They could have been Hellenistic Jews, Gentile proselytes to Judaism, or simply Greeks who made their home in the territory of Galilee. The fact that we are not told the identity of these people suggests it is not important for us to know who they were.

We know these folks were going up to Jerusalem along with God-fearing Jews to worship at the Passover Feast. Also, we are told they wanted to see Jesus, but why they wanted to see Him is not said. For whatever reason, instead of going directly to Jesus, they went to Philip who was from the Galilean area. They told him they were desirous to see Jesus but apparently did not tell him why either. Philip did not go to Jesus directly but instead went and told Andrew of the Greeks' request. Then both Philip and Andrew went to Jesus with the request.

John does not tell us whether the Greeks actually talked to Jesus personally or not. So the question remains unanswered. Did they or did they not ever have a private audience with Jesus? It seems from what He said after being informed of their request that He answered the questions they intended to ask to Him.

We must remember that Jesus came into the world to be Israel's Messiah and the world's Savior. At this time He was still reaching out primarily to the Jews. The coming of these Greeks or Gentiles seems to have prompted Him, however, to announce that His hour had come, that He would soon go to the cross, die for the sins of all, and through His death be glorified.

Jesus' Troubled Soul, vv. 23–27

Maybe you think Jesus should have responded to the request from the Greeks through Philip and Andrew with a "yes" or "no" answer. Instead, Jesus spoke of the hour for which He came into the world. To the two disciples and all who would listen He talked about how a grain of wheat that is planted or falls into the ground must first die before it can sprout and eventually bear fruit. This was His way of answering the question the Greeks wanted to ask about.

The mission His heavenly Father had sent Him on must be completed. He must die and He did willingly give Himself as a Substitute for all. Before Jesus could be resurrected from the grave and glorified, He must die on the cross.

The Savior also explained how the main purpose in life ought to be to please God. His death on the cross pleased His Father. In the Father's plan Jesus would be both the Sacrifice and the Sacrificer for all the sin of all mankind. He said the one who hates his life in this world shall keep it to life eternal" (v. 25). What did Jesus mean by this? Surely, He did not mean His followers should be morbid and suicidal. He did mean though that what is must important in life is not to please self but to please God.

Now my soul has become troubled," Jesus said (v. 27). No doubt this was because He was once again reminded of the awful cost of our redemption. This was His emotional response to the cross. He then asked a question which was directed to Himself and to those to whom He was speaking. The question was, "What shall I say, Father, save Me from this hour?" Quickly He answered the question with, "But for this purpose I came to this hour" (v. 27). The cross was the greatest tragedy in the world and the greatest victory at the same time.

The Father's Voice from Heaven, vv. 28–33

Always, Jesus wanted the Father's name to be lifted up, to be praised, to be glorified. He had come to do the Father's will. He had humbled Himself to be man and to always do His Father's will, not reluctantly, but joyfully. We too, as God's children, should always have as our ambition, no matter what the circumstances are, that God would be praised and honored by the way we live.

Jesus prayed as He ministered to the Greeks who had come to see Him and the Jews around Him. What was His prayer? "Father glorify Your name" (v. 28) was His request. The answer from the Father came quickly assuring Jesus that He had been glorified and would continue to glorify His name.

As He had done before, God made His voice heard. The silence of heaven had been broken. Not only did Jesus hear it, but the people around Him heard it also. They were not sure what that which they heard was. Some said it was simply a clap of thunder. Others said an angel had spoken (v. 29). Jesus told those who heard the voice why it was given. It was not for His sake but for theirs (v. 30).

The voice of God the Father from heaven was also heard at the baptism of Jesus early in His public ministry (Mark 1:11). Again, that voice was heard at the transfiguration of Jesus before three of His disciples (9:7).

As Jesus anticipated the cross, He spoke of it as though what He would do there through His death was already accomplished. When He died, He took the sinner's place, died as the sinner's Substitute. At this same time He judged Satan, He defeated him. Proof of this is the resurrection of Jesus from the grave. This was God's declaration that the death Jesus died was accepted by the Father as payment for man's sin. Of course, that finished work must be received, appropriated, by sinners or it does not benefit them. Those who reject Jesus' payment for sin are condemned therefore by it. Those who receive it by faith are declared righteous before God the moment they believe.

Jesus made sure everyone hearing Him, including the Greeks, would know that when He would die on the cross, He would die for all, not just for Jews. That must have been good news, expecially for the Greeks. On the basis of His finished work He draws all to Himself. Verse 32 of John 12, the key verse, describes Jesus' anticipation of the cross. Their eternal destiny depends upon how they respond to that drawing, that conviction.

The People's Question of Jesus, vv. 34–41

How striking, those who were excited to accept Jesus as the "King of Israel" (v. 13) were soon not accepting Him as the crucified King. They apparently got His message about being lifted up—a message of crucifixion. They were not at all sure this was the Messiah predicted in their Scriptures.

In other words, they were happy to accept Jesus as a King who would deliver them from Roman oppression but not as their Deliverer from sin. After all, they reasoned, the Messiah would reign forever (Psalm 89:4; Ezekiel 37:25). Who is this Son of Man who was going to be lifted up? They were confused and did not understand the limited nature of their revelation. Jesus told them they needed to trust Him as the Light of the world and live in His light or revelation (John 12:35). They needed to believe what He said and not withhold faith until they fully understood. We need to do the same.

Having reminded them who He was, Jesus departed from the people and hid Himself from them. This means He would defend His claims before these unbelieving Jews no longer, at least not at that time. John, led by the Spirit of God, brought Isaiah's teaching in alongside what Jesus was saying and doing. His point seems to have been to illustrate how the rejection of Jesus by His own people should not surprise people acquainted with the Old Testament Scripture. John quoted from Isaiah 6:9–10. This quotation shows again how dangerous it is to harden one's heart, to disbelieve God. He often adds hardness to hardness as in the case of Pharaoh. Happily, not all who heard Jesus on this occasion disbelieved in Him. Many, even some among the rulers, did believe Him as we shall see.

Secret "Followers" of Jesus, vv. 42–50

Those who did believe in Jesus chose to remain anonymous. Why? It was because they feared the Pharisees. What was it that caused them to fear these religious leaders? Why should they be afraid of the Pharisees? It was the same thing that caused the blind man's parents to refuse to tell them all they knew about their son and how Jesus gave him sight.

Remember what the parents said to the Jews who questioned them? "Ask him; he is of age, he will speak for himself" (9:21). John adds, "They did this because they feared the Jews would put them out of the synagogue. Now that same fear fell upon some of those very Jews. They too could not think about being put out of the synagogue. These Pharisees had an awesome grip on everybody. Thus these believers became secret followers of Jesus. They, John said, loved approval from men more than approval from God (v. 43). That is so sad! It is still sad today when the same sin is committed. Why is it that we so often fear man more than we fear God?

It seems that Jesus reached out again to those who rejected Him and to those who only saw Him as a national Deliverer. To do that He stressed once again how terrible it was to disbelieve Him (vv. 44–50). What He said on this occasion were His last words to the people at large, these whom He earlier said He came unto but was not received by most of them (1:11).

Jesus "cried out" His message on this occasion. This was another expression of His troubled soul (v. 27). Many times before, He had said the same thing, heralded the same message. The heart of that message was no one can have God as his heavenly Father who does not have Jesus as his Savior. To reject Him is to reject the Father. The only way to the Father is through Jesus the Son.

In this loud cry Jesus reminded His hearers once again that He was the Light of the world. He who rejects Him rejects the One who sent Him. Those who do this must bear God's judgment. Jesus did not come to bring judgment but to bring salvation. In a future day the Savior will be the Judge, however (5:22). Everything Jesus said and did was at the direction and discretion of the Father.

Personal Applications

This portrait of Jesus anticipating the cross serves as a final reminder that what He said of Himself and His relation to the Father from the beginning of His public ministry was still true. How man responds to Jesus and His work on the cross determines his or her eternal destiny.

Jesus' reference to how a grain planted must die before it can grow and bear fruit should remind us how important it is to let go of self and put God first. We can never be fruitful for God until we turn ourselves over completely to God and allow His Spirit to control us and work through us. We must die to self before we can be effectively used of God. How very important it is for us to realize that being a child of King Jesus means more than escaping hell. It means also that God expects us to be His disciples, His followers.

Time flies by so swiftly. We should remind ourselves frequently that only what's done for Christ will last. Opportunities to serve come and go. God would have us buy up every opportunity, redeem the time, to represent Him in our daily lives in our homes, in our places of employment, and in the market place. We need to work while it is still day. The night comes before we know it.

Jesus had His eyes set on Calvary. In this portrait we saw Him anticipating the costly cross. We too must keep the cross and open tomb before us always. This will compel us to sacrifice and do service for our Lord.

Study Questions

1. Who were the secret followers in this study?

2. How did Jesus respond to the Greeks' request? Why?

3. Why was Jesus troubled?

4. What was significant about Jesus' attendance at this Passover Feast?

5. How was Satan related to Jesus' cross work?

6. What does God want us always to keep before us?

7. What specific changes do you plan to make in your life as a result of this portrait of Jesus? When will you begin to make those changes?

Washing Feet

Portrait 18

John 13:1–20

As Christians it is so easy to forget that we need regular cleansing from the defilement of sin. Without this, our fellowship with God and our service for Him are hindered. Like our Lord's disciples, we need to have our feet washed too. Jesus washed His disciples' feet as a lesson for them of their need for daily cleansing from sin.

The spiritual cleansing they needed and we need does not come from water. Jesus drew upon the example of physical water to illustrate for them and by application for us the need of staying in fellowship with Him. The way to do this is to allow God's Word to keep us clean. The psalmist learned that, didn't he? To God he said, "Your word I have treasured in my heart, that I might not sin against You" (Psalm 119:11). Another important thing to remember is that when we sin, we need to admit to God that we have. That is what the apostle John meant when he wrote, "If we confess our sins, He [God] is faithful and righteous to forgive us our sins and to cleanse us from all unrighteousness" (1 John 1:9).

Demonstrating our need to keep short accounts with God, to experience daily cleansing from sin, John has given us this portrait of Jesus, washing the disciples' feet. Let us examine it and see how we can benefit and learn from it.

The Occasion for the Washing, vv. 1–3

This portrait of Jesus introduces us to what has come to be called Jesus' Upper Room Discourse (John 13–17). The discourse proper is in chapters 14 through 16. However, the foot washing experience recorded in chapter 13 serves to prepare the disciples for the instruction given in chapters 14 through 16. And in Jesus' High Priestly Prayer in chapter 17 He prays home the truths He taught them in the Discourse.

There is some disagreement among Bible believers as to which day Jesus was crucified. Some believe it was on Wednesday. Some are certain it was on Thursday. Most, however, believe He was put to death on Friday. If that is the day, and there is convincing support for it, then the Upper Room Discourse was given on Thursday evening.

Jesus, of course, was fully aware of His approaching arrest, trials, and crucifixion as well as His resurrection and ascension. He knew His hour had come. Nevertheless, He continued loving His disciples. He loved them to the end, John tells us. This Upper Room setting was the last time Jesus would be with His disciples before His death. He knew that, but the disciples most likely still were not sure about it.

Some time during the Passover Supper the devil put into Judas Iscariot's heart the plan to betray Jesus. What a striking contrast in this portrait. The love of Jesus for His own and Judas' decision to betray Him to His enemies are glaring opposites. It reminds me of a jeweler placing a gorgeous diamond on a black velvet cloth to bring out its beauty and even its size.

It seems certain that at least a major reason for the foot washing was because the disciples had been arguing about which of them was the greatest (Luke 22:24–27). It appears that this argument took place at the beginning of the supper while they were taking their places around the low table around which they would recline. Each of them seemed to think they deserved the place of honor at the table, near Jesus.

Earlier, James and John made a request through their mother for places of honor in the kingdom (Mark 10:35–45). Sounds like these men were revealing a normal human behavior. They were seeking first place and arguing with each other, even at such a sensitive time. But we do the same so often. God help us to get and stay humble. Hopefully, examining this portrait of Jesus will assist us in that direction.

Jesus knew who He was and why He had come into the world. He knew too that after the completion of His mission on earth He would return back to the Father. All authority had been committed to Him by the Father. He knew that also (5:27). Because He knew all these things, He also knew that no condescension would or could diminish His authority. He therefore proceeded to wash the disciples' feet.

The Example for the Washing, vv. 4–5

Jesus got up from the low table where they all ate in observance of the Passover. He took off His outer garment but kept His tunic on. This was normally what servants wore (Luke 22:27). Then He wrapped a linen towel around His waist and secured it by knotting it loosely. This allowed Him to have both hands free to carry the basin of water and wash the disciples' feet. With the towel He also dried their feet.

In the Near East where this all took place footwashing was an important task. The people wore sandal-type "shoes," and the sand and dusty walk-ways made the washing necessary. The washing was most likely just dipping one's foot into the water and then drying it. Many hosts had a servant at the entrance who would provide this service for guests. We cannot determine for sure from the account whether or not the disciples washed each other's feet as they entered the Upper Room. It seems most likely that they had not done this, especially since they had been talking, in fact arguing, with each other as they made their way to the Upper Room as to who would be the greatest in the kingdom which they expected Jesus to establish.

When Jesus got up from the table and got the basin and water, the disciples may have thought He was going to carry out the ritual of ceremonial washing of the hands (v. 5). To help you remember this portrait, try memorizing this verse. They soon found out that was not what He was going to do. Whose feet did He wash first? The text does not say. The answer is most likely related to the order of the disciples around the table. Because of Peter's response when Jesus came to him, he most certainly seems to have been first.

The Need for the Washing, vv. 6–11

In his typical knee-jerk way, Peter put up serious resistance when Jesus knelt before him to wash his feet. Peter's surprise, his shock, at the thought of Jesus washing his feet was robust. Both words "you" and "my" in his response are very emphatic. "Lord, do you wash my feet?" He said to Jesus. Peter's reaction at this time reveals that he did not understand Jesus' upcoming death and therefore certainly not the meaning of it. It appears he was almost speechless. And that was most unusual for him. Peter had earlier expressed his faith in Jesus as the Christ, the Messiah, the Son of the living God (Matthew 16:16). In view of this, imagine Jesus doing now what slaves usually did. That is what this portrait is all about.

It is interesting to observe how Jesus responded to Peter's question. He did not offer any explanation. He simply told Peter that what He was about to do was not for him to know then. The significance of it would become clear later. The obvious thing Jesus wanted Peter to do was to simply trust Him even though he did not understand. That is what God wants us to do many times. Sometimes faith must precede understanding. "Hereafter" Jesus told Peter he would understand. In fact, during the interchange with Peter, Jesus explained in part at least what His act meant (v. 10). Was Peter trying to display humility in the way he responded to Jesus? If he was, he failed miserably. Instead he displayed enormous irreverence toward Jesus. With sternness Peter said, "Never shall you wash my feet" (v. 8). The answer Jesus gave Peter must have frightened him. In essence, Jesus told him unless He would wash his feet, he would lose fellowship with Him. They would no longer have much in common. Peter then quickly said, in effect, if that's the case, wash me all over. He was beginning to get the picture but still did not understand the difference between a relationship with Jesus and fellowship with Him. Jesus proceeded to explain the difference to him.

The two different verbs Jesus used in His response to Peter are very significant. He said, "He who has bathed needs only to wash his feet, but is completely clean; and you are clean, but not all of you" (v. 10).

"Bathed" was used by Jesus to refer to Peter's relationship with Jesus, his salvation. The word refers to washing the entire body. As Jesus used it here, it referred to Peter's acceptance of Him as Savior. "Wash" in Jesus' answer is from a different word and referred to cleansing a part of the body. Peter along with all the others in that Upper Room, except Jesus, needed regular washing from the defilements of sin. Ever since, all who know Jesus as Savior need the same. This washing has to do with fellowship with God. No one can be saved, redeemed, twice. The bath of regeneration is received once for all at the moment of faith. However, all of us need daily cleansing of defilement from sin. The source for both the "bath" and the "washing" is the same. It is the cross-work of Jesus.

We learn more about who Jesus was referring to when he told Peter that one among them was not clean, had never been born again. He it was who would betray Jesus. Did Peter understand what and who Jesus was referring to? Probably not, but we cannot be sure about that. He may have had some hints.

The Explanation for the Washing, vv. 12–20

After washing the disciples' feet, Jesus took His place again at the table. In that culture they reclined at the table leaning on one elbow with their legs outstretched behind them. Jesus had already explained the meaning of what He had done to Peter. When He got back to the table, He asked the other disciples if they knew what He had done to them. Jesus answered His own rhetorical question. In doing that, we might say He gave the practical application of His washing their feet. Only after His death and resurrection would they more fully understand, however.

To begin, Jesus reminded the men how they referred to Him—Teacher and Lord (v. 13). When they called Him Teacher, they were acknowledging His authoritative teaching. Calling Him Lord implied they were recognizing His authority over their lives. From their custom, Jesus drew the conclusion they should have already known—if that's who I am to you, you too should wash each other's feet (v. 14). Jesus had given them an example of humility which they were to follow. Washing the disciples' feet illustrated Jesus' willingness to serve. They too should do the same.

Some today choose to believe that because Jesus used a custom of the day to illustrate humility and servanthood, the same example should be practiced today as a local church ordinance. Unless great care is taken in the insistence of actual washing of others' feet, pride can result while seeking to obey Scripture. The same is true of any way we seek to live humbly. If we are not careful, we will commit the sin of being proud of our "humility," whether we believe Jesus taught this footwashing or not.

The primary point Jesus wanted His disciples to get was that they were His servants and He was their Lord. That order must never be reversed. It is just as true now as it was then. God's people, all of them, must never say or do anything which gives the impression that they are greater than the One who sent them.

Frequently, all of us need to be reminded of what Jesus did in this portrait which John has painted for us. He, the Lord of glory, first of all humbled Himself to become one of us. Then throughout His entire life on earth, He demonstrated how His followers should live. Though we are children of the King of kings and Lord of lords, we are always only servants saved by the Savior.

Before Jesus identified the betrayer He referred to earlier, He gave a promise to His own. Obedience to what He had just visibly taught them would bring divine blessing. He made it very clear though that the promised blessing was only for those who are truly His. This clearly eliminated

Judas. Jesus allowed him in the group "that Scripture may be fulfilled" (v. 18). The Scripture He spoke of was Psalm 4:9. The verse reads, "Even my close friend in whom I trusted, who ate my bread, has lifted up his heel against me."

The final word in this portrait was from Jesus to the disciples. Jesus said, "I am telling you this before this dastardly deed is committed so that when it is carried out, you will remember and know I am He."

Personal Applications

Have you washed anyone's feet lately? I do not mean with a basin, water, and a towel. I mean have you demonstrated a truly servant role to someone in need. There may be people all around you who have lost their way. Maybe some have become bitter, perhaps even toward God. Do you know someone who is depressed and has poor self-esteem? You might be used of God to be the one He wants to don the servant mentality, to take specific steps, to even go out of your way to wash the feet of someone.

God, of course, will not write your name in the sky and give directions there. Neither will He whisper His desire for you in your ear. He has already spoken in His Word about our responsibilities toward others. "Bear one another's burdens" (Galatians 6:2) is a clear mandate for us. Repeatedly, Scripture describes believers as servants, bondslaves, and Jesus as Lord and Master. We must never forget the servant is never above his or her Lord. That is what Jesus stressed as He washed His disciples' feet.

Perhaps, for whatever reason, you do not often hear of someone who is hurting and needs help. Your church leaders or Bible class teachers would more than likely know of many with special current needs. They would be happy to direct you to them, put you in touch with them.

Study Questions

1. What led Jesus to wash the disciples' feet?

2. How did they respond to His wishes?

3. What major lesson did He teach through His action?

4. Why did the disciples need their feet washed?

5. How do you expect to carry out Jesus' exhortation to His disciples this week?

Identifying His Betrayer

Portrait 19

John 13:21–38

JESUS HAD just finished giving a supreme example of humility and a short discourse on the important relationship between Himself as the Master and the disciples as servants. As we examined the portrait of Jesus washing the feet of the disciples, we found applications for our own lives. In that portrait there was obviously a closeness and sense of unity and seriousness between Jesus and those He had called to be His disciples. There was, however, one of these men who in reality had already determined to betray the Lord.

Immediately after Jesus had said to the twelve, "He who receives Me receives Him who sent me" (v. 20), He revealed His upcoming betrayal. The one who would betray Him had not received Him. That meant the betrayer had not received God the Father either. Had not Jesus repeatedly told the Jews who were determined to silence Him that they could not have God as their Father if they rejected Him [Jesus]? Now one of the twelve was in view as one who had not received Him. Instead, he was about to betray Him.

Betrayal of some one close to you is especially heart-rending. When it happens to us, we look back and reflect on things he or she said, did not say, or do and wonder why we did not see the betrayal coming. On the other hand, we sometimes see it coming and are not totally shocked when it takes place.

In the case before us in this portrait of Jesus the one who would betray Him was not suspected by the other disciples to be one who would do such a thing. Even still today we all have some unanswered questions about the entire incident. We will not find answers to all our queries as we analyze the portrait; but it is hoped we will at least come to a better understanding of this horrible behavior and how Jesus appealed repeatedly to Judas Iscariot before he betrayed Him.

The Revelation of Jesus' Betrayal, vv. 21–25

The Son of God was so human that He was "troubled in spirit." This means He was disturbed emotionally. We are not told whether He was troubled because of the betrayer or the disciples or both. All we know is Jesus experienced anguish of soul. He was deeply troubled.

Try to imagine how the news that one of them would betray Him must have sounded to the eleven and to Judas.. They perhaps thought they had not fully understood what Jesus said. "What did He say?" they may have said to each other. When they were sure they understood, they began looking at each other in amazement to try to find out whom precisely He was talking about.

Finally, Peter, in customary fashion, decided to have John ask Jesus whom He was referring to. Who among them would do such a thing? We do not know for sure the "seating" arrangement around the table. We can only be certain that John, "whom Jesus loved" (v. 23), was beside Him to the right since he was "reclining" on Jesus' breast.

John, of course, was one of the three disciples in the inner circle. The other two were Peter and James. Jesus truly loved all His disciples, yet John was especially close to Him. Five times in his Gospel, John described himself as the one whom Jesus loved (13:23; 19:26; 20:2; 21:7, 20).

Perhaps we need a bit more information about the culture of that day so we can understand some things that seem strange to us. To begin, the table was probably only about twelve or fourteen inches high. There were no chairs around this table either. People usually reclined on a pillow or sat on a mat when reclining. Their legs were stretched behind them away from the table. They would lean on their left elbow if right-handed or on their right elbow if left-handed.

Most likely Peter was directly across the table from Jesus because he gave some gesture to John to ask Jesus who it was who would betray Him. We are told in John's account that after receiving the message from Peter, John leaned back closer to Jesus to ask Him, "Lord who is it?"

The Revelation of the Betrayer, vv. 26–30

Jesus responded to Peter's question with, "That is the one for whom I shall dip the morsel and give it to him" (v. 26). This key verse clearly describes this portrait. After saying this, Jesus dipped the morsel and gave it to Judas who must have been close by. Somehow John must have given Jesus' identification of the betrayer to Peter. It is doubtful that anyone else around the table heard the messages between Peter and John.

Maybe something similar happened when Judas asked Jesus a question after He made His announcement that one of the group would betray Him. Matthew records this question from Judas and Jesus' answer. "Judas who was betraying Him, said, 'Surely it is not I, Rabbi?' Jesus said to him, you have said it yourself" (Matthew 26:25). If any of the other disciples had heard what Jesus said to Judas, they would have known Judas was the betrayer.

The custom was for the head of the group observing the Passover Feast to dip a morsel, a piece, of either bread or meat into a dish of broth or sauce before eating it. Jesus did this and gave it to Judas. And, in fact, Judas most likely took the place of highest honor which would have been on the left side of Jesus. Many see what Jesus did by dipping the morsel and giving it to Judas as well as allowing him the place of highest honor at the table as an opportunity for him to change his mind about betraying Jesus.

Jesus gave Judas several clear appeals and warnings on this very occasion. He washed his feet (vv. 5, 12). And Judas heard the announcement that one of the disciples was not clean (vv. 10–11). Jesus quoted from Psalm 41:9 about one who would eat bread with Him and yet lifted up his heel against Him (v. 18). Specifically, Jesus said in Judas' hearing, "One of you will betray me" (John 13:21). The morsel or sop was handed to Judas by Jesus (v. 26). When Jesus got no response, He sent Judas out with the words, "What you do, do quickly" (v. 27).

Judas was truly a master of deceit. Those who ate with him, slept with him, and followed Jesus with him did not suspect him. At least we have no record that they did. Only when they got to the Garden of Gethsemane and saw Judas with the band of soldiers did they realize the significance of all Jesus' appeals and warnings to him. Even when Jesus dismissed Judas from the group, the disciples had no idea what he was about to do. Since Judas was the treasurer of the group, they suspected he was going out to buy food for the Feast of Unleavened Bread which began the day after Passover.

The Revelation to the Disciples, vv. 31–38

The timing of what Jesus said to the remaining disciples is most significant. No sooner than Judas had left the group to negotiate with Jesus' enemies, Jesus said, "Now is the Son of Man glorified, and God is glorified in Him" (v. 31). These words reveal a sense of relief from Jesus. Judas' departure was for Jesus the recognition that His death, resurrection, glorification, and ascension were in essence completed. Judas had refused to heed the repeated warnings and opportunities Jesus gave him. The dye was cast. True, the actual crucifixion when He would bear in His body the sins of all men of all ages, including Judas', was still hours away. Yet in the mind of Jesus the work was already virtually accomplished.

God the Father and Jesus, God the Son, were glorified in Jesus' coming, in His work on earth, and in all He did at Calvary and the open tomb. There is here a strong inference of Jesus' glorification, ascension, and being seated at the right hand of the Father where He ever lives to make intercession for His people (cf. Philippians 2:8–11 and Hebrews 1:3).

Jesus used a most tender and compassionate term to describe the eleven disciples. He used this term only this one time though John used it frequently of those to whom he wrote the Epistle of 1 John. The term "little children" (v. 33) would more accurately be "little born ones." This expression displays a deep affection and kinsmanship for these disciples despite their immaturity.

Earlier, to the unbelieving Jews Jesus said something similar, and yet very different (7:33–34; 8:21) from what He said to His little born ones (13:33). To His critics Jesus said that where He was going they could not come and in fact would die in their sin. The striking difference is that, yes, Jesus would be separated physically from the eleven, but He was going to prepare a place for them, and He would always be with them in spiritual union (14:1–3, 18, 23). Though they probably did not fully understand what this meant, they should have found some comfort in it.

The next thing Jesus said as He sought to prepare the eleven for their work after His return to the Father concerned a new commandment (v. 34). That new commandment was that they should love one another. Had these men not loved one another? Why give them such an admonition on the eve of His crucifixion? The Mosaic system, with which they were very familiar, told them, "Love your neighbor as yourself" (Leviticus 29:18). Jesus had also already said, "You shall love your neighbor as yourself" (Mark 12:31). James, Jesus' half-brother, called the old commandment the "royal law" (James 2:8).

The law of the Mosaic system called for loving one's neighbor as he or she loved himself or herself. The "new" commandment which Jesus gave was to love as He loved them. That was a sacrificial love. It was a special love for the unlovely. Also, the new commandment was based on a family relationship within the family of God. The love called for earlier was based on the covenant relationship with God.

Loving one another, Jesus said, would be the way those who had not yet received His love for them would mark them and us off as Jesus' followers, His disciples. Pagan writers did in fact observe the loving relationship which the early Christians had for each other. Felix, for example, wrote, "They love one another, even before knowing one another."

Upon hearing Jesus' call for loving one another, Peter, perhaps speaking for more than himself, asked Jesus where He was going (v. 36). It appears that the Lord knew Peter really wanted to go with Him and that was why he asked the question. Parents can identify with such a "where" question from their small children. Behind the question is the desire to go with the parent wherever it is, except of course if it is to the dentist.

Being the Son of God, Jesus knew what Peter was thinking. Jesus did not tell him specifically where He was going but said Peter could not follow Him on this journey at that time but would follow later. In some ways Peter was a sincere but slow learner as we shall see.

After Jesus told Peter he could not go where He was going at that time, Peter asked why he could not go with Jesus right now. It seems clear that Peter wanted to be with Jesus. He did not want to be separated from Him. And in his typical bold fashion Peter made another one of his promises. It was one similar to what he said when Jesus prepared to wash his feet. You shall never wash my feet, he assured Jesus (vv. 8-10). But, of course, Jesus did wash his feet. Here just before Jesus would be arrested, tried, and crucified, Peter again says, "I will lay down my life for you" (v. 37). What a bold promise that was. Did he do that? No, at least not at that time though history does record that later he died a martyr's death. Before his death Peter did stand out in his defense of Jesus in the Garden of Gethsemane. He drew his sword and cut off the ear of one helping to arrest Jesus (18:10–11).

Jesus' answer to Peter's well-meaning, and I am sure well-intentioned, promise was, "Will you really do that, Peter?" "You," Jesus said, "will deny me three times before the rooster crows in the early morning" (v. 38). And of course that is exactly what happened (Luke 22:54–62). I cannot help but wonder how Peter in his mind responded to what Jesus told him.

Immediately after Jesus' arrest, the soldiers took Him to the house of the high priest. Peter followed at some distance and was approached first by a servant-girl who saw Peter sitting by an open fire with some of Jesus' fiercest critics. She said to those around her, "This man was with Him too" (Luke 22:56). Peter quickly denied the charge and said he did not even know Jesus. A bit later another person saw him and said to Peter directly, "You are one of them too" (v. 58). Again, Peter vehemently denied that he knew Jesus. About an hour later the third denial came from Peter when a third person said Peter was with Jesus and he was a Galilean. As Peter was denying the third time, the rooster crowed (v. 59), just as Jesus said it would.

Jesus turned and looked at Peter. Then he remembered the prediction Jesus made about his denial of Him. How did Peter respond to this sad reality? He did what all of us need to do when we have failed, when we have sinned. Peter went out and wept bitterly (Luke 22:62). The words both Matthew and Luke use to describe Peter's response to the convicting look from Jesus describe strong crying (Matthew 26:75; Luke 22:62). The words denote a loud, boisterous crying. Peter realized he had sinned; he failed his Lord.

Personal Applications

Judas is a reminder to us to be sure we are not just pretending we have received Jesus as our Substitute for sin. He fooled and surprised a lot of people but not himself or Jesus. Each of us must realize no one is born the first time gradually. Physical birth is not an ongoing process. There was a time when we entered our earthly family. It is the same with God's heavenly family. No one gradually becomes a child of God. Being born again takes place at a point in time. We may not remember the exact date, but we should know that we have trusted Jesus alone as our Savior and passed from death into life. Judas never had that experience which all the other disciples had.

Jesus did not want Peter to die for Him at that time. He really wanted Peter to live for Him. Sometimes our problems seem so huge that we want to just die and go to be with Jesus. Wonderful as it will be to see Him face to face and be with Him forever, we must remember He has work for us to do here. He has little lambs which need to be loved and fed by us. Our times are in His hands. It helps too to remember when the load seems hard to bear, God will never call upon us to be anything or do anything without equipping us for the task.

Study Questions

1. What do you think Jesus thought when He decided to tell the disciples one of them would betray Him?

2. How do you think Judas felt when he heard those words from Jesus?

3. Do you have any ideas why the other disciples were so slow to suspect Judas?

4. Why do you think John was especially loved by Jesus? Was his relationship with Jesus his idea or Jesus'?

5. Have you ever been betrayed by a close friend?

6. Can you remember any of the things Jesus did or said which should have reminded Judas that Jesus loved him? Look for them in John 13:21–28.

Healer of Broken Hearts

Portrait 20

John 14

IN THE Bible there are dozens of references to the word "heart" in both the Old and the New Testaments. A few samples from each Testament will help us understand what is meant by the use of this term. We are told that "the intent of man's heart is evil from his youth" (Genesis 8:21). The psalmist wrote of the meditation of a person's heart (Psalm 19:14). He prayed that God would create in him a clean heart (Psalm 51:10). "The joyful heart is good medicine" (Proverbs 17:22). Jesus said, "Blessed are the pure in heart" (Matthew 5:8). He also spoke of the hardness of the heart (Matthew 19:8). He told the disciples just before He departed from them to return to His Father, "Let not your heart be troubled" (John 14:1). With the heart man believes, Paul declared (Romans 10:10). He also reminded the Christians at Philippi to guard their hearts and minds" (Philippians 4:7).

How are we to understand the meaning of the word "heart" from references like these? Was the human organ that pumps blood and therefore life throughout the body in view? Obviously not. None of the above references describe the physical human heart. Instead, what is meant in all of the above references is human intent and desire. Throughout Scripture, "heart" refers to the seat of human emotion. It is a description of the real person that no one but God can see completely. But surely each of us knows when our heart is not right with and about others.

As we look at this portrait of Jesus, we will see Him as the One who can and wants His own to have attitudes and motives that are pure and honest. Jesus will soon be experiencing death on a cruel Roman cross. The description beneath this portrait finds Him giving last minute words to His disciples. They have very serious unanswered questions which they are asking Him. They simply do not understand what is going on. What is going to happen to Jesus? Where is He going? Why can they not go with Him? How can He be our King if He is going to die?

As Jesus responds to their questions, we will see Him as the Healer of their broken hearts. This same Jesus wants to be the Healer of our hearts when they are broken.

Peter's Questions, 13:36–14:4

Occasionally we need to be reminded that the chapter and verse divisions in the Bible were made by men, not God. Most of them seem correct and help us understand the units of thought. However , the division between chapters 13 and 14 of John seems to be a bit confusing.

Peter asked Jesus, "Where are you going?" (13:36). Jesus answered, "You can't follow where I'm going but you will follow me later." Peter asked a second question, "Lord, why can I not follow You right now?" With that he added, "I will lay down my life for you" (13:37). Jesus responded to that bold well-meaning promise of Peter by telling him he would in fact deny Him soon.

Not only to Peter but to the other disciples present as well, Jesus said, "Let not your heart be troubled" (14:1). This promise from Jesus makes this verse key. Jesus told the remaining disciples He would leave them and where He was going they could not come at that time. It was this startling statement that brought great consternation to them. Their hearts were indeed troubled. They were terribly distraught.

Jesus spoke to them about their troubled hearts. What we have in 14:1 is still part of His answer to Peter who spoke for the rest in 13:33-38. With love, Jesus literally commanded these men to stop letting their hearts be troubled. The second part of His command was that they should keep on believing in God and keep on believing in Him, Jesus. Their troubled hearts weakened their faith in God the Father and in Jesus His Son.

What was true then for those disciples is just as true today for all of God's children. When our hearts are troubled, we have less faith in God. The reverse is also still true. When we have strong faith in God, our hearts remain calm even in the fiercest storms of life.

Thomas' Question, 14:5–7

It must have been a bit discouraging for Jesus to hear how little of what He taught the disciples was really learned. All of us are often slow to understand the things of God. We need to be patient therefore with Thomas.

His question to Jesus was in essence, "We don't even know where you are going, so how can we know how to get wherever it is You are going?"

The answer that Jesus gave to Thomas must have startled him. He may even have been more confused than before he asked his question. We may assume Jesus and Thomas were facing each other during the interchange between them. Jesus said to Thomas, "I am the way, and the truth, and the life" (v. 6). What an answer that was! Jesus did not say He told people about the way, though He did. He did not say He told the truth, though He always did. Neither did Jesus say He told people about life, though He did. Rather, what He said was that He personified the way, personified the truth, and personified life.

Jesus then added, "No one comes to the Father but through Me" (v. 6). That must have gotten Thomas to thinking, "But I have come to the Father through faith." It appears that this man was confused. He has been called "doubting Thomas." Interestingly, he was the first of Jesus' disciples to say he was willing to die with Jesus (11:16) yet the last among them to believe He had risen from the dead (20:24–28).

We do not want to be too hard on Thomas, however. It does seem though that he had a rather earthly and temporal view of things at times. He appears to have understood virtually everything Jesus, Israel's Messiah, taught in terms of the material kingdom. Because of his earthly perspective, Thomas had no clue where Jesus was going. This man Thomas displayed a rather materialistic attitude of which many of God's people are guilty. You? But, Jesus did choose Thomas, knowing all about him. He did so to help him. And He did! He has and will continue to do the same for us.

Thomas not only did not know Jesus fully; he did not know God the Father fully either. Knowledge of the One brings knowledge of the other, Jesus told Thomas. Jesus also assured him that from that point on he would have a fuller, deeper knowledge. That prompted the question from Philip.

Philip's Request, 14:8–21

Obviously, Philip was listening in on the conversation between Thomas and Jesus. In fact, Philip had to be quick to get a word in, no doubt, before Thomas would say something else. Philip did not get it any more than Thomas did. "Show us the Father, and it is enough for us" (v. 8), Philip said. Though not a direct question, it was one that was surely implied. What is the Father like? Can you tell us more about Him? Also, implied but not stated, Philip was saying, "We never saw the Father, like we have seen You."

Perhaps Philip was thinking about how Moses had a deep desire to see God. And God did show Himself to Moses, at least in a limited way. We cannot help but wonder, "Would that have satisfied Philip and the rest of the disciples?"

Once again, Jesus reviewed for Philip, and whoever else was there, that He and the Father were equal and of the same divine essence. He had taken on humanity but the Father had not. The Father was and is spirit without a physical body. Jesus told Philip that He was in the Father and the Father was in Him (vv. 10–11).

We must be sure to understand that Jesus did not say He and the Father were the same Person. Each one is a separate Person though each is of the same divine essence. Their union was and is a spiritual one. In coming to this earth, Jesus took a subordinate position but not a subordinate essence. He did not become less than God. Jesus reminded His disciples in this portrait to believe Him, to accept by faith what He said. If they needed some visible assurance of Jesus' equality with God, they were told to believe Him because of His miraculous works. Both the words and the works of Jesus revealed the Father.

God the Father was and still is revealed through His people. Jesus assured the disciples of this. After He would ascend back to the Father, they would do even greater works than He had done, greater, that is, in number, not greater in kind. God's people are left here to be revealers, lights, and even salt, to make God known to those who do not know Him.

There was still more in Jesus' response to Philip's request. Philip wanted to know more about God the Father. Jesus told him He was God's Revelation and Revealer. His words and works gave testimony to that. God the Father is also shown through the lives and testimonies of His people. The final part of Jesus' answer to Philip's request was concerned with the Holy Spirit, the Third Person of the Godhead, the holy Trinity.

Jesus assured His disciples and all of God's children by application, that the Holy Spirit would be their divine Helper. The Holy Spirit would come and continue the work which Jesus began. He would come in alongside them and help them. This Helper, this "Spirit of truth" (v. 17) would reveal truth, testify to it, and defend it. The Holy Spirit, Jesus said, would be with the disciples and in them.

It must have been very assuring for these men to hear Jesus say that He would not leave them as orphans. The world of mankind who did not know Jesus would not see Him after He left this earth. The disciples would not see Him either with their physical eyes. But with the eye of faith they would see Him and sense His presence with them through the work of the Holy Spirit.

Judas' Question, 14:22–26

This is not Judas Iscariot. The Judas mentioned in this portrait of Jesus is also called Thaddaeus (Matthew 10:3). There is no record of any other question asked of Jesus by any of the disciples before Jesus was crucified. About the same time that the Judas in John 14:22 asked Jesus this question, Judas Iscariot was bargaining to betray Jesus. What a contrast between these two.

What Judas wanted to know was how Jesus was going to manifest Himself to the disciples and not to the world (v. 22). Perhaps Judas thought Jesus had changed His plan. The words Judas used indicate he wanted to know what had happened. The question arose in Judas' mind when Jesus said the world would soon see Him no more but the disciples would (v. 19). Three ways by which Jesus would be manifested or disclosed to the disciples but not to the world form His answer to Judas' question. We may assume the same question was on the minds of the other disciples also.

Jesus' Counsel, 14:27–31

First, Jesus promised those who love Him would keep His word and both He and His heavenly Father would make their abode with that person. Certainly, this is reference to the spiritual presence of God the Father and God the Son and not a physical presence. Only God's people would in this way have God manifested to them.

Second, Jesus promised God the Holy Spirit would also manifest, disclose, Jesus to those who love Him. The Third Member of the holy Trinity would come and teach the disciples all they needed to know and bring to their remembrance all that Jesus had taught them. In other words, they would be given divine assistance. This part of Jesus' answer to Judas really amounts to Jesus authenticating the New Testament books which His disciples would later write.

Third, Jesus assured His disciples and all who would receive Him until the end of time, by application, the gift of God's peace. This marvelous gift includes first of all peace *with* God and is a reality when Jesus alone is received as personal Savior. Second, those who have peace *with* God need to experience the peace *of* God continually. As they live out the

Christian life, this peace, Paul tells us, "surpasses all comprehension" and "will guard" our "hearts and minds in Christ Jesus" (Philippians 4:7).

So, Jesus really is the Healer of broken hearts. How does He do this? He does it in response to our faith in Him. At the very beginning of our look at this portrait of Jesus He urged His true disciples, Judas Iscariot being absent, to not allow their hearts to be "troubled" (v. 1). Now we listen in as He tells the same men the same thing again with the added word "fearful" (v. 27). They and we therefore have the responsibility to put an end to a troubled and fearful mindset.

Personal Applications

Georgia Stiffler put the message of this portrait very succinctly and Phil Kerr arranged the music in "Healer of Broken Hearts."

Verse 1:

Is your life full of heartaches and sadness?
Are your dreams all shattered and torn
There is One Who through mercy and suff'ring
For you every sorrow has borne.

Verse 2:

Do the threads of your life seem so tangled,
That you wish you had never been born?
There is One Who is willing to help you;
He knows every sorrow you've borne.

Chorus:

He's the healer of broken hearts;
He'll mend your shattered dreams.
He'll pick up the threads of your broken life,
  and weave them together again.
To your soul He'll bring peace and joy;
  your friend in need He'll be.
The healer of broken hearts,
  is Jesus of Galilee.

Study Questions

1. Do you think it was proper for the disciples to ask Jesus the questions they did?

2. There was one "where" question, one "what" question and two "how" questions. Who asked these of Jesus?

3. Why do you think the disciples were troubled and fearful?

4. Who is the other helper Jesus promised?

5. What three things did Jesus stress in His counsel to the disciples?

6. Make a short list of things that trouble you and make you fearful. Make another list of things you can do to experience the peace of God.

True Vine

Portrait 21

John 15

JESUS AND His eleven true disciples left the Upper Room where He had washed their feet and taught them of their need to serve Him humbly. Judas Iscariot had already gone out to bargain with Jesus' enemies in order to betray Him. For thirty pieces of silver he did just that. In this beautiful portrait, John was directed by the Spirit to use the metaphor of the vine and the branches to teach the disciples the great truth of their identification, their union, with Him and the need to abide in Him to be of service for Him.

These words of Jesus to the eleven were spoken to them the last evening before His crucifixion. It seems highly likely that Jesus presented Himself and them in this metaphor as He was walking with them toward the Garden of Gethsemane. Vineyards were a very common sight for the disciples, and Jesus may have drawn attention to them as they left the city and He began to speak of Himself as the true Vine. These men would have also been familiar with the Old Testament teaching that Israel was like the Lord's vineyard but failed to bear much fruit. The prophet pictured Israel as an "empty vine" (Hosea 10:1). Jesus may also have gestured to the sculptured vine on the temple gate as He said, "I am the true Vine" (v. 1). Here is the key verse setting forth the full meaning of this portrait.

Also, we should remember that they had just celebrated the first observance of the Lord's Supper together. The fruit of the vine in the cup was doubtless a preliminary preparation for what He would say to them about Himself as the true Vine and they as branches. They, however, probably did not make the connection between the two until much later.

The New Testament epistles have a lot to say about the close relationship between Jesus and believers. It speaks about the believer being in Him and He being in the believer. Here, before those books were written, we have a very vivid picture of the union of the believer with Jesus. Also, in this portrait we see the tremendous importance of the believer's abiding in Jesus. To put it another way, by way of application, this portrait sets forth a twofold emphasis—union with Jesus and communion with Him.

Three great truths stand out in this portrait about Jesus and His people. The first is the certainty of the believer's union with Christ (vv. 1–17). The second is the certainty of the world's hatred of the believer (vv. 18–25). The third is the Holy Spirit's help for the believer (vv. 26–27).

The Certainty of the Believer's Union with Christ, vv. 1–17

Union and communion describe the relationships between the true Vine and the branches in these verses. Union between Jesus and believers is described by two words—"in me" (v. 2). The communion of the believer with his Lord is in the form of a command: "abide in Me" (v. 4).

Every time representatives of the nation Israel tried to find some fault in Jesus so they could discredit Him before the people, He spoke of His relationship with His heavenly Father. The disciples had heard those accusations and Jesus' response to His critics.

He is alone now with those He had chosen to be His eleven disciples. Jesus will soon be crucified by those same accusers, and He must assure His own of His union, His equality with the God of the Old Testament. He does this metaphorically by calling Himself the "true Vine" and His Father the "vinedresser." The eleven disciples were, and all believers since, are united to Him and His Father just as the branches are to the Vine. Jesus did not say He was a vine He was *the* true vine in contrast to all other vines.

There are two kinds of branches stemming from the vines at which they were probably looking. There were those branches that were not bearing grapes and those that were productive. The lesson Jesus was teaching was very pointed. Those "branches," or believers in Him, who were not bearing fruit "He takes away"; and those bearing fruit "He prunes" so they bear more fruit. Both kinds of branches were in Him just as there were both kinds of branches in the natural vines. So there are two kinds of branches and two different kinds of response from Jesus to them.

The Vinedresser, whom Jesus has identified as His Father, "takes away" those branches not producing fruit. Those branches bearing fruit He "prunes" so that they will bear even more fruit. The progression of fruit bearing in this portrait is both interesting and challenging. First, some branches have no fruit on them. Second, there is "fruit" on other branches.

Then as a result of pruning there is "more fruit." And finally in response to abiding in Jesus the true Vine there is "much fruit" (vv. 2, 5).

We must keep in mind as we look carefully at this portrait that both kinds of branches are united to the vine. It is important to ask therefore, What is the meaning of "takes away" those not productive and "He prunes" those which are productive?

The Greek word translated "takes away" is from the root word for resurrection—to raise up. As the vinedresser walked through his vineyard, he would lift up those branches which had no fruit and expose them to more sunlight so they would bear fruit. The same word is used in John 8:59 to describe how those opposed to Jesus "picked up stones" to throw at Him.

This means that when God the Father, the Vine-dresser in this account, sees a branch, a believer, not bearing fruit, He gently assists that person by encouraging him or her of their need. Discipline for such does come if there is no positive response from the Father's helping hand. But first there is assistance and encouragement. He comes to the rescue of sinning Christians. What wonderful news that is!

What about the pruning of the branches already bearing some fruit? The word "prunes" means cleans. The vinedresser does this often and continuously. Both the vinedresser in the account and God the Father, the spiritual Vinedresser, carry on this important work. This is done so the branches and believers as branches will bear even more fruit.

Jesus reminded the eleven to whom He was speaking that they were already clean or pruned (v. 3). Furthermore, He told them how they had been cleaned or pruned. It was through the word which He had spoken to them. For all believers beyond the eleven disciples, by way of application, the means by which they are continually cleaned or pruned is the same— the Word of God. David the psalmist speaking of the precepts, the commandments of God, said, "By them your servant is warned, in keeping of them there is great reward" (Psalm 19:11).

Following the teaching of the *union* of Jesus with the believers comes the instruction on the need for the believer to be in *communion* with Jesus.

Abiding in Jesus is the responsibility of each believer. God brings each one into union with Him in response to faith in Jesus as the One who paid the full price for our sin. The command from Jesus to "abide in Me" means as God's children we are to be continually in communion, in fellowship, with Him. God's work unites us with Him. It results in an eternal relationship with Him. As we abide in Him, we enjoy fellowship with Him. How do we abide in Him? John tells us, "the one who keeps His (Jesus') commandments abides in Him" (1 John 3:24). These would involve all He taught recorded in the New Testament.

Unless we abide in Jesus, we cannot bear fruit any more than a branch can bear fruit without abiding in the vine. As we look carefully at this portrait of Jesus, we discover a number of wonderful results of abiding, of being in fellowship, with Jesus. First, when we abide in Him, He abides in us (v. 4). Second, we bear fruit, our lives are productive for Him when we abide in Him (v. 5). Third, He gives us special enablement to serve Him. Apart from this abiding, we can do nothing that counts in heaven's records (v. 5). Fourth, abiding in Jesus assists us in our prayer life (vv. 7, 16). Fifth, God the Father is pleased and glorified when we abide in His Son (v. 8). Sixth, we experience a special portion of divine love as we abide in Jesus. Seventh, unspeakable joy floods the soul of those who abide in Jesus (v. 11). Finally, John tells us that when we abide in Jesus, we will begin to understand His great love for us. This, in turn, will enable us to love one another, even those who are not easy to love (vv. 12–17).

The Certainty of the World's Hatred of the Believer, vv. 18–25

There was no question about what Jesus meant when He told the disciples, "If the world hates you, you know that it hated Me before it hated you" (v. 18). All the portraits of Jesus which John painted for us have hidden in them, and sometimes not so hidden, the hatred of representatives of Satan's world system. The construction in the Greek New Testament of the words "if the world hates you" is known as a first class condition. This means the hatred was assumed to be true at that time. Jesus made the fact of the world's hatred of the believer certain, in other words. Before Jesus ever went to the cross, the representatives of Satan's *cosmos*, world, despised and abhored both Jesus and His disciples.

You might ask, Why was that so? It was because neither Jesus nor the disciples were of the world. Both were in the world as lights; He the Light, they reflections of that Light, but not in sympathy with its anti-God stance. They were therefore not of it. Neither embraced the philosophy of the world.

The disciples needed to be reminded that as Jesus' servants, they were not greater than He who was their Master. The hostilities which were poured out on and toward Jesus would very soon be poured out on His own as well. And they were. History records that many of them, if not all, were martyred for their faith. Everything that would happen to them by way of persecution would be because they so closely related to Jesus and all He stood for, His "name's sake."

Then, as now, there are many who claim to believe in God and at least in time of trouble want to claim a relationship to Him. However, those who hate Jesus and want nothing to do with Him hate the Father also, Jesus said (v. 23). He then appealed to Psalm 35:19 and 69:4 which say, "They hated Me without a cause." Originally, the psalmist was writing about himself and those persecuting him. Jesus, however, applied the psalmist's words to Himself and His followers.

Our world is becoming increasingly more hostile to those who stand for truth. We live in a pluralistic society and post-modern culture where absolute truth is denied; it is nonexistent. Those who embrace this philosophy of life believe it is narrow and bigoted to believe, for example, that Jesus is the only Way to heaven and home. These people do not care what you believe just as long as they can believe what they want to believe. They refuse, however, to believe Jesus is *the* Way, *the* Truth, and *the* Life or that no one can come to God the Father except through Him (14:6).

The Certainty of the Holy Spirit's Help for the Believer, vv. 26–27

It should have been a great encouragement to the disciples to know Jesus would not leave them as orphans in the world. To be sure, He would soon ascend back to the Father who had sent Him to the world. After His departure He would send the Holy Spirit, the Third Member of the holy Trinity. The Spirit who existed eternally would begin a new ministry in the world. He would come as the Helper, the Comforter, the Paraclete. The Spirit's principle work in the world was to continue what Jesus had begun. That, in fact, is still His work in our world. The Holy Spirit is one of the same kind as Jesus, equal in His deity to that of the Father and of the Son. He would be sent by both the Father and the Son. He would bear witness of Jesus. And He did and still does.

Personal Applications

How can we apply the truths of this portrait to our own lives today? What is there about Jesus as the true Vine, revealed so long ago, that can make a difference in the way we live in the twenty-first century?

Here are a few suggestions for you to think about and try to carry out in your home, where you work, and among your friends and associates. Jesus revealed the true vine portrait of Himself to the eleven disciples for their benefit. He wanted to help these discouraged, despondent, downcast disciples to carry on triumphantly after His return back to the Father. They desperately needed His help.

Each of us needs His help also. Our world is not a friend of grace; it never was and never will be. Our culture is very different from theirs but most of the same difficulties confront us that faced them.

On a regular basis we need to remind ourselves of the certainty of our spiritual union with Jesus as His children. We are just as much in Him and He in us as was true of those men long ago.

The organized system headed by the devil which leaves God out, or in other words, the world, is still our enemy. The world hates us just as much as it hated the disciples because they and we both love Jesus.

The Holy Spirit is our Helper also. He indwells each believer permanently. He seals and strengthens each of us. The Spirit's primary work is to exalt Jesus and He wants to do that through us. He guides each believer and expects us to respond properly to His leadership.

We must never be too busy to have time with God. Each of the three suggestions above involves God's Word, the holy Scriptures. Its teaching regarding our position before God, our responsibilities toward others, must be appropriated and reaffirmed on a regular basis.

Study Questions

1. What do you think prompted Jesus to use the vine and branches which make up this portrait?

2. What three great truths are stressed in this portrait of Jesus?

3. How does Jesus treat branches in Him that do not produce fruit?

4. How does His treatment of the branches bearing fruit differ?

5. Why did the world hate Jesus?

6. Why does it hate believers today?

7. What is your plan for carrying out the three great truths of the portrait?

Promise-Maker and Keeper

Portrait 22

John 16:1–15

PROMISES ARE easy to make but often are much harder to keep. Sometimes we fully intend to keep a promise we made, but for reasons beyond our control we cannot do what we said we would do. Or maybe we just forget we even made the promise.

Are you not glad God always keeps His promises? And there is never an instance when something unforeseen comes up and He simply cannot fulfill His promise.

Young children often promise parents a lot of things about their future behavior and then so quickly forget. As God's children we often do the same thing. Thank God for His loving forgiveness in times like these. Thank Him too that when He gives us a promise in His Word, He will always fulfill that promise.

In the portrait of Jesus which John painted for us today Jesus promised the coming of the Holy Spirit and His ministries in the world. There is no question about it, Jesus is the Promise-maker and Keeper in John 16:1–15. We want to observe carefully why the new ministry of the Holy Spirit was needed, what that new ministry is, and how extensively it is reaching us today.

The Need for the New Ministry of the Holy Spirit, vv. 1–6

Jesus had just finished telling the disciples how they would be hated by the world. He reminded them they, as His followers, were not "of the world" but had been chosen by Him to be witnesses in the world. The world hated Him and it would therefore hate them also because they loved and served Him. Those who hated and persecuted Jesus would do the same to His disciples. Whether those who hated Jesus and His followers knew it or believed it or not, they were at the same time hating God the Father.

Those doing the hating may not realize this, but it is still true. But the divine Helper, the Holy Spirit, Third Member of the holy Trinity, would come, Jesus said, and help them bear witness about Jesus in a very hostile environment.

The disciples probably did not fully understand all that Jesus was telling them. The reality of His coming death, resurrection, and ascension back to the Father and His physical absence from them had not yet had its full impact on them. Today we would say they were still in a denial mode. But they must be prepared for what lies ahead for them. Jesus knew to be forewarned was to be forearmed.

The unthinkable would become reality. They would be cast out of the synagogue. Those who would kill them would think they had done God a service. This sounds like some religious fanatics in the world today, does it not? Why would the religious leaders among them do such things to them? Jesus said, because "They have not known the Father or me" (v. 3). They knew about God the Father but did not know Him. There is a lot of difference between the two.

There was another reason for the new ministry of the Holy Spirit of God. Coming persecution, and even death, certainly made necessary the coming of the Holy Spirit. Added to that was the fact that Jesus would no longer be physically with them to help them during those very hard times.

Jesus did not want His disciples, to whom He would soon give solemn responsibilities, to stumble. They were told later to "make disciples of all the nations" (Matthew 28:19). This was and still is an awesome assignment. And they would need to do this without Jesus' physical presence and in an ever-increasing hostile world as well.

Here we see Jesus preparing the eleven disciples for what they would face as they served Him. They must never forget not only that He had told them about the hard times ahead but also that the Holy Spirit would come and help them do their work.

Once more, in this portrait, Jesus said, "I am going to Him who sent Me" (John 16:5). His statement, "None of you asks Me where are You going?" raises a question. Peter had asked a form of the question earlier (13:36). What did Jesus mean then by His accusation? It seems certain that He was bringing to their minds that none of them had asked anything about His return to the Father and what all that meant. They were interested primarily, if not solely, in their own loss and not of His gain. They were, in other words, acting childishly. Young children often cry when their parents go away and usually it is not because of where they are going or even what they will do, but just that they are leaving them.

The eleven were so wrapped up in themselves that they showed little concern about Jesus' glory but were only thinking of their loss. Later, after Jesus had ascended back to the Father, they did return to Jerusalem with great joy (Luke 24:52)

The New Ministry of the Holy Spirit, vv. 7–15

God the Holy Spirit is as eternal as God the Father and God the Son are. The Person and work of the Holy Spirit are set forth many times in the Old Testament Scriptures. But the Holy Spirit began a new ministry when Jesus had finished His work on the cross and had risen from the dead and returned to the Father. The Spirit was sent by both the Father and the Son to the earth to continue what Jesus began. This does not mean all His earlier ministries ceased when He was sent into the world. No, but He did begin special and new ministries.

The Holy Spirit was sent by Jesus. He told the disciples that if He would not leave them, the Spirit would not come. Jesus' work on earth was finished. The Holy Spirit needed now to do His work in and through Jesus' followers. He has, and still has, an indispensable work to do in the world which advances the work Jesus began.

Jesus' promise to the eleven is very specific and definite. Speaking of the Holy Spirit, He said, "I will send Him to you" (v. 7). We can find great hope from this key verse. And, of course, Jesus kept His promise. The Holy Spirit came and began His ministries in the world. What Jesus promised the Spirit would do in the world is indispensable to the work Jesus' followers are to do. Without the Spirit's work, they could not do their work.

The Holy Spirit was sent into the world to do three specific things to the people who populate the world. Jesus said when the Spirit comes, he will convict the world of sin, of righteousness, and judgment. You see, the world of mankind has completely wrong ideas about sin, righteousness, and judgment. The Spirit of God has been sent, as Jesus promised, to set mankind straight, as it were, on these three counts. He has other important ministries as well, but these three are the ones highlighted in this portrait of Jesus.

The words "convict" (v. 8) and "conviction" mean to present unquestionable and demonstrable proof. Jesus promised not only that He would send the Holy Spirit to help His followers. He also promised that the same

Holy Spirit, the divine Helper, would give to mankind, those to whom they would share the good news, unquestionable proof of the truth of the gospel. This means that Jesus' followers were not given the responsibility of convicting people of the truth of the gospel message. Their task was to present, to announce, the good news of the gospel. They, and in turn we, have the responsibility to be good-news carriers, sharing the message as ambassadors for Jesus. The conviction and regenerating work has always been the Spirit of God's. That in itself is good news, is it not?

First, the sinner needs to know he or she is in a state of sin. Why is that the case? It is because "they do not believe in Me" (v. 9), Jesus said. Condemnation now, and eternally outside of Christ, is because of refusal to accept Jesus' payment for sin and the sinner. Those outside of Jesus will be outside of heaven because His payment for their sin was not received and, therefore, was rejected (John 3:18).

Second, Jesus promised the Spirit would give unquestionable proof to humans everywhere, to the "world" of the righteousness of Jesus. He promised this because, the only truly righteous One on earth, was raised from the dead and would ascend back to the Father. Man generally has a totally wrong understanding of righteousness, thinking it can be attained by oneself. The divine righteousness of Jesus was fully vindicated when He was raised from the dead. The Spirit's work in the world as promised by Jesus in this portrait of Him is to convince humans they need to be clothed in His righteousness to enter heaven.

Third, the Holy Spirit, Jesus promised, would give proof beyond any doubt of the certainty of God's judgment upon sin and sinners who reject Jesus. Proof that this judgment was true is that the "ruler of this world" (v. 11), Satan, would be and has been judged at the cross

How, we may ask, does the Spirit do this convicting of sin, righteousness, and judgment? We are not told specifically how He does it but only that He does it. It is reasonable and in harmony with Scripture to believe God the Spirit does His work promised by Jesus through the proclamation of His Word—preached, shared in word or song or some other means. But how does He do it where the Bible's message has not been available? Perhaps He does it in those places through God's revelation of Himself in nature and human conscience. Those who receive that message as God intended, He sovereignly brings the gospel message. Of this we can be very sure, the Spirit has come and does precisely what Jesus said He would do whether we can explain how He does it or not.

So far in our study of Jesus as the Promise-maker and Keeper, we have observed why we need the new ministry of the Spirit, promised by Jesus.

Also, we have seen that this ministry concerned Jesus Himself since His return to the Father made the Spirit's ministry necessary. In this portrait of Jesus' promise of the Holy Spirit's help, His conviction of the world of this great truth of the gospel formed a big part of this portrait.

Two more descriptions of the promised Spirit's new ministry must not escape our notice. First, Jesus assured His own that the Spirit would guide them personally " into all truth" (v. 13). That should have been a tremendous encouragement to them. My, how they needed supernatural assistance to carry out the assignment given to them. The Spirit, Jesus assured them, would not exalt Himself but rather would exalt Jesus and continue the work He began. Furthermore, the Spirit would disclose to them things to come (v. 13).

Second, the Spirit would glorify Jesus. He would "take of Mine and shall disclose it to you" (v. 15). How does the Spirit do this? As the believer is led by, controlled by, and empowered by the Spirit, Jesus is glorified. The Holy Spirit teaches the "things" of God the Father and of God the Son and gives God's people, not just the clergy, an understanding of them (v. 15). This is another way of saying the Spirit takes the Word of God and from it He teaches the yielded person, the teachable, the things of God.

Personal Applications

Do you sense a need for the Holy Spirit's work of revealing Jesus to people? Sometimes we have a hard time understanding why people we know and share the gospel with do not seem to get it. In times like these, remind yourself your job is to be the good-news carrier, to share clearly and lovingly the gospel message. Our assignment is not to try to bring conviction to people. We must allow the Holy Spirit to do that through the Word we share. Our task is to give people the good news. It is the Holy Spirit's work to do the convicting, drawing, and regenerating—giviing them eternal life.

It is a good idea to remind ourselves periodically about the last two things Jesus promised the Spirit would do. Remember He fulfills all His promises–always. First, He said the Spirit would guide us into all God's truth and second, He would glorify Jesus through us. Of course, both of these things require our involvement. We must expose ourselves to God's Word regularly and feed upon it spiritually. Likewise, we must be involved in sharing that Word with our lives and our lips if we expect to bring glory, praise, and honor to Jesus.

Study Questions

1. Why did the disciples of Jesus need the new ministry of the Spirit?

2. How does the departure of Jesus from His disciples relate to that new ministry?

3. What three things did Jesus promise the Spirit would do toward the world of humans?

4. List some ways you can use the message of this portrait of Jesus in your life.

5. Think about someone to whom you plan to share the gospel this week. Plan your strategy ahead of time and pray that the Spirit will guide you.

Predicting His Death, Resurrection, and Ascension

Portrait 23

John 16:16–33

SOME OF the things that Jesus told His disciples in the portrait we looked at from John 16:1–15 troubled them. What concerned them most was not what Jesus said about the new ministry of the Holy Spirit to come. At least they did not ask anything about that. What puzzled these men was that Jesus said He was going to physically leave them (v. 7). Shortly after saying that, He said He would depart from them and they would not see Him, but then in a little while they would see Him again (v. 16). In this way Jesus summarized this portrait. That makes the verse key.

These whom Jesus called to be His close followers were very ordinary men. They had some of the same doubts and difficulties of understanding that we have. The Savior needed to instruct them line upon line and precept upon precept, as it were. Jesus did not leave them in a state of confusion but explained what He meant by what He said. Through the teaching ministry of the Spirit He will do the same for us. He is our divine Teacher who helps us, when we are yielded to Him, to understand the deep things of God.

Do you know of anyone who predicted when he or she would die, who would be responsible for the death, the way they would die, and that they would be raised from the dead three days later? Jesus did all of that and more concerning His death and resurrection and it all took place just as He said. This portrait of Jesus allows us to see and believe that He was truly the Son of God.

Let us take some time gazing at this portrait of Jesus. As we do, we will learn how He helped His bewildered disciples and encouraged them to face the future without His physical presence with them.

Predicament of the Disciples, vv. 16–18

Because they expected Jesus to establish His kingdom on earth and rule the world from David's throne in Jerusalem, the disciples could not understand what Jesus meant about leaving them. At least five different times He told them clearly that He was going to leave them and not be with them in the flesh.

At the time of the footwashing in the Upper Room He said, "Little children I am with you a little while longer . . . where I am going you cannot come" (13:33). "If I go and prepare a place for you, I will come again and receive you to Myself," He told them (14:3). On the same occasion the disciples heard Jesus say, "You heard that I said to you, I go away, and I will come to you" (14:28). From the portrait of Him as the Promise-maker and Keeper we heard Him say, "But I tell you the truth, it is to your advantage that I go away; for if I do not go away, the Helper will not come to you; but if I go, I will send Him to you" (16:7).

Once more as He began to speak of His death at the hands of the Jews and His resurrection in the portrait we are examining now, Jesus added "a little while" and you will see Me (v. 16). Interestingly, John used two different words for "see" in verse 16. The first "you will no longer *see* Me." The second in the phrase "and again a little while, and you will *see* Me." The first "see" emphasizes the physical act of seeing. Very shortly after Jesus said this, He was taken out of their sight when He was betrayed and arrested in the Garden of Gethsemane. However, He was raised from the dead three days later and appeared and talked with His disciples. They did see Him again. It seems the disciples' uncertainty had reached its peak. The prediction about not seeing and again seeing Him had not yet occurred.

Some of them brought their confusion out in the open, "What is He telling us?" they said to each other. "What does He mean by "a little while" between His going and His return to us and we will see Him? Also, the disciples did not know what He meant about "going to the Father."

I wish we knew who among the eleven were expressing their predicament. Knowing what we do about Peter, he may very well have been the ring leader and the first to broach the subject. It is likely too that James and John may have been in the huddle as well. But we cannot be sure about this, and it does not really matter. We do not need to know, but the way John records the incident, it appears that all in the group were in the dark, as it were. "We do not know what He's talking about," they said (v. 18).

Prediction of Jesus, vv. 19–22

They did not know, but Jesus did know what was bothering them. How did He know that? Did He simply overhear their discussion? Maybe so, but there is nothing in John's account to support that. Rather, this was another example of Jesus demonstrating His omniscience, His complete knowledge of all things, to these frustrated disciples. Jesus knew what they were thinking and saying without actually hearing it. He was not eavesdropping on them. Instead He was demonstrating that He was all He claimed to be, very God of very God. He knew what these men could do, would do, might do; He knew it all.

Proof of Jesus' complete knowledge is in His question to them. He repeated the concerns voiced by those who had been discussing what Jesus had said to them about not seeing and seeing Him again. Then He responded with more specifics about the hardships they would receive from the world and how those who would cause all the persecution would rejoice at what they could do while the disciples would weep. Jesus illustrated the outcome of their future sufferings and joys by appealing to how a woman is in great pain and then has great joy when her child is born. He promised the eleven they would eventually have joy that no one could take away from them.

Prayer in Jesus' Name, vv. 23–30

Prayer was not something new to the disciples. Their knowledge of the Old Testament teaching and examples on the subject was not lacking. Too, Jesus prayed and called upon them to pray. Prayer was not a new thing to them. What would be new about it was how it was to be done when Jesus would not be with them any longer. During the three years of their service with Jesus they went to Him directly for everything they needed. But He would not be with them much longer. The disciples probably did not even think about how they were to ask God for things or go to Him with praise after Jesus would no longer be with them physically.

This whole issue of prayer for the disciples while He was away from them was among the last things Jesus taught them before His death. Jesus' instruction on this subject was greatly needed. After He would be gone from them, they would realize how very important it was for them to know how to pray.

Up until the time Jesus was talking to the disciples about how to pray, they had asked for nothing in His name. They simply came to Him directly with all their needs. Jesus told them that in the future they would be able to go to God the Father directly and make their problems and requests known in Jesus' name. In fact, He promised them that whatever they requested of God He would give them, if they asked in Jesus' name. No longer would it be necessary for them to come to Him and then He would make their request known to the Father. That was all to change after Jesus' death, resurrection, and ascension back to the Father.

Because God the Father loved the disciples and because they loved Jesus and believed He came from the Father, the disciples would be able to go directly to the Father with their requests. But we must ask, What did Jesus mean by making requests to the Father in His name? The phrase "in Jesus' name" after our prayers often becomes a mere polite way of concluding our prayers. That certainly is not what Jesus meant by the instruction to His disciples. "In Jesus' name" means on His merit. It means to ask in harmony with His work and will. Simply concluding prayer with the phrase "in Jesus' name" without regard for what Jesus would ask in this case amounts to forging His name to our wishes. Only prayers prayed in harmony with Jesus are heard and answered by God the Father. He knows our hearts and is not fooled by spiritual forgeries. God's answers to our requests are not always "yes" and not always "no." Many times His answer is "wait."

Promise of Scattering, vv. 29–33

That they would be scattered and leave Jesus alone must have been some of the saddest news the eleven had ever been given. There was much they did not understand about what Jesus had already told them, but this news? Of course, the news that Jesus was going to leave them and not be with them physically was shocking. But Jesus did tell them He would send the Holy Spirit to be their Helper and He would further the work that Jesus had begun. That was surely good news. And how about the fact they would soon be able to go to God the Father directly with their needs, worship, and praise? That was more good news in the midst of some that made them sad.

When Jesus explained the figurative language He had been using as He taught the disciples, they said, "Now we know that you know all things. . . . by this we believe that You came from God" (v. 30). That expression of faith was good as far as it went.

However, Jesus raised some question about it. "Do you now believe?" He asked them (v. 31). There should be no doubt that the faith of these men was genuine. It was real and true as far as it went. They had not yet had their faith put to the test, however. Even though Jesus had told them about how they would be hated and persecuted because of their relationship with Him, there were things about the future they did not know. Perhaps these men were a bit self-confident just as we often are.

Jesus told them plainly that they would be scattered each one to his own home. In fact, they would forsake Him leaving Him alone with His heavenly Father. In the midst of the sad news there was a promise of peace if they would abide in Him. They could have peace in the midst of war from the world. "Tribulation?" (v. 33), yes. There could be no doubt about that. But neither could there be any question about the peace which He made available to them.

The word "tribulation" referred to here is the very same word used to describe the "scattering" (v. 32) of the disciples. This word was used to describe how sheep are scattered when wolves attack a flock (10:12).

The tribulation referred to here describes the same trouble and trials believers have always experienced in their pilgrimage. It does not describe the future time of unprecedented tribulation of the coming Great Tribulation in fulfillment of God's promise of the outpouring of His wrath in the seventieth week of Daniel 9:24–27. God has not promised that the Christian life will be a bed of roses without thorns. He did not promise this to the eleven or to any others. He did, however, promise deliverance from the divine wrath to come. The apostle Paul put it this way, "Jesus, who rescues us from the wrath to come" (Romans 1:9). And again he said, "God has not destined us to wrath, but to obtaining salvation through our Lord Jesus Christ" (Romans 5:9).

Personal Applications

It is so good to know that Jesus knows it all. Is it not? He knew what His disciples were troubled about, what they did not understand, and He knows all about us too. We humans learn line upon line, precept upon precept, but our God and Savior knows all things about everything. He does not learn as He relates to us. He even knows what could have been, but never came to pass.

This total and complete knowledge of God is both wonderful and fearful; it is comforting and convicting. When no one seems to understand, He knows our hearts, our true motives, and desires. By the same token, He knows all about the sins we hide from everyone else and wish we could hide from Him.

Perhaps as a result of our study of this portrait, we will be more mindful when we close our prayers with "in Jesus' name." As believers we address God as our heavenly Father, we pray in the power of the Holy Spirit, and we pray in Jesus' name. We should not demand anything from God. We come to Him on the merits of Jesus. What a wonderful privilege it is to come to the very throne of God boldly because of what Jesus has done for us.

Christians in the USA have been spared many persecutions that Christians in other parts of the world experience. We need not look for persecutions for our faith, but the closer and truer we are to Jesus, the more likely we are to be persecuted in one form or another. We need what the disciples of Jesus needed—to claim the promise, take courage, Jesus has overcome the world.

Study Questions

1. What have you learned or come to better understand from studying this portrait of Jesus that you did not know before?

2. What things did Jesus promise His disciples in this portrait of Himself?

3. What does it mean to pray in Jesus' name?

4. One outstanding attribute or characteristic of Jesus stands out in this portrait. What is it?

5. How do you think your faith may be tested this week? How do you plan to respond?

Praying for Himself

Portrait 24

John 17:1–5

ARLIER WE have called John 13–17 the Upper Room Discourse of Jesus. In chapter 13 we saw Him washing the disciples' feet. We now want to listen in as He prays after His instruction to the disciples in the Discourse proper. John 17 is truly the Lord's Prayer. Here He is in intimate communion with His heavenly Father. Listen as He prays.

We are not altogether sure where the Savior was when He prayed this intercessory prayer. It seems most likely that He and the disciples were on the way from the Upper Room to the Garden of Gethsemane. He prayed as they crossed the Kidron Valley to the slope of the Mount of Olives. Some do think, however, everything in chapters 13 through 17 was said and done in the Upper Room.

Imagine it. Jesus, the very Son of God, in prayer on the eve of His arrest and crucifixion. Our Lord's deity did not diminish His need to pray. It is beyond our full comprehension that He as God the Son found it necessary to pray. This is not the only record we have about Jesus' prayer life. He prayed often and even taught His disciples how to pray (Matthew 6:9–13). What we have in Jesus' prayer of intercession is no doubt a window into His many prayer times. This is, though, the most extensive prayer recorded telling us precisely what He prayed for.

Here are some examples of times and places when and where Jesus prayed. None of these, however, tell us what He specifically prayed for. He prayed when John the Baptist baptized Him in the Jordan River (Luke 3:21). When He began His public ministry on earth, He prayed (Mark 1:35). Before He chose the twelve disciples, He prayed all night (Luke 6:12). On the Mount when He was transfigured before the three disciples there, He prayed (Luke 9:29). In fact, it was as He prayed on that occasion, that He was transfigured. While dying on the cross, Jesus prayed (Luke 23:46).

The prayer of Jesus recorded in John 17 is in three parts. He prayed first for Himself, then for His disciples, and then for all who would in the future believe on Him because of the message from His disciples.

The portrait of Him praying for Himself is the one we want to look at now. In the next portrait we will see Jesus as He prays for His disciples and for all those who would believe on Him and become His disciples, and that includes every believer to the end of time.

Let us examine three aspects of our Lord's prayer for Himself: His approach in prayer, His appeal in prayer, and His authority in prayer.

His Approach in Prayer, v. 1a

Actually, Jesus' approach in this prayer is twofold. After speaking to His disciples at length about His upcoming death, resurrection, return to the Father, the Holy Spirit as their Helper, and His own return to take His own to the place He promised to prepare for them, Jesus turned to His Father in prayer.

In lifting up His eyes to the heavens He said, "Father" (v. 1). Here is our key verse to help us remember this portrait. What an approach in prayer that was. To call God His "Father" speaks of His dependence upon Him and His need for Him as He carried out His work on earth. That must have thrilled the heart of God to hear that word "Father" from Jesus.

There were actually six times in this prayer that Jesus addressed God as His Father, which of course means that He was the Son of God. This tells us Jesus was affirming, in the hearing of the disciples, that He was of the same divine essence as the Father. Jesus is never called the child of God in the Bible but always the Son of God. In verses 1, 21, and 24 the address is simply "Father." "Holy Father" was His address in verse 11 and "righteous Father" in verse 25.

It is important that Jesus called upon God the Father at this crucial time. His approach was not to call on the disciples who were with Him. Not even His mother or any of the holy angels could have assisted Him. Only His heavenly Father was called upon to meet His need. This very first word in Jesus' prayer demonstrates His submission and dependence on the Father.

The second part of Jesus' approach in prayer is closely related to the first part. The hour has come," He said. Never were glory and gloom so closely related as they were when Jesus died. The "hour" He was referring to is not a period of sixty minutes but the time when He would bear in His own body all the sins of all mankind as He became mankind's Substitute for sin.

Six other times this "hour" is referred to in John's Gospel. Jesus referred to this "hour" as He ministered on earth. To Mary His mother He said, "My hour has not yet come" (2:4). John the apostle said Jesus' "hour" had not yet come (7:30). And again he said the same thing when His enemies tried to seize Him; they could not because it was not the Father's time (8:20). Then later, certain people wanted to see Jesus, but Jesus said, "The hour has come for the Son of Man to be glorified" (12:23). On the same occasion Jesus declared, "Now my soul has become troubled and what shall I say, Father, save Me from this hour? But for this purpose I came to this hour" (12:27). Just before the prayer we are looking at now, Jesus said to His disciples, "Behold an hour is coming, and has already come, for you to be scattered, each to his own home, and to leave Me alone, and yet I am not alone, because the Father is with Me" (16:32).

Jesus' death on the cross was not only His "hour." It was also God the Father's "hour" because He gave His Son to die for sinners. It was also the "hour" for His people, those who would be part of His heavenly family. Since Jesus died as the Lamb of God who took away the sin of the world (1:29), He made provision for whosoever will receive Him as their Substitute for sin. Finally, in a very different sense, the "hour" Jesus would die was also Satan's "hour." It was there on the cross that Jesus defeated Satan and conquered death. Satan was judged by Christ when He became mankind's Substitute for sin.

Jesus' Appeal in Prayer, v. 1b–3

This too was made in two parts. The first appeal was "glorify Your Son," and the second, "that the Son may glorify You." Let's look at these two separately.

"Glorify Your Son" was a prayer for the Father's support while Jesus was on the cross. The purpose for which Jesus came into the world climaxed at the cross and the empty tomb. With great confidence, therefore, He prayed that upon His return to the Father's side He might enjoy in His very presence all the glory of heaven. Before Jesus ever was born of Mary, He enjoyed this glory. Even before the world was created, in which creation He had a vital part, He enjoyed this glory. But now in anticipation of His work on the cross and resurrection from the grave the glory to be restored and enjoyed would even be greater than before. Why? Because the work He was sent to do was finished. Mankind had been provisionally reconciled to God and now each individual must accept Jesus' substitution to be personally reconciled to God.

This appeal from Jesus to God the Father was also a request for the Father to grant adoration, majesty, and honor through His Son's death. The apostle Paul recorded the answer to this request of Jesus (Philippians 2:9–11). The "hour" of human tragedy was to be an "hour" of divine triumph, and it was. Jesus did not appeal to the Father to have the world give Him glory, praise, and exaltation. He did want the Father to grant Him this glory.

Jesus' request to be glorified was so that through His own glorification the Father would also be glorified. We know this because Jesus said, "Glorify Your Son, so that the Son may glorify You" (v. 1).

As in His life on earth, so in His death, Jesus wanted only to do those things that pleased and honored His Father. Always, God the Father was preeminent in His thinking. He said He always did those things that pleased the Father. This was uppermost in His mind. Jesus wanted the same through His death.

Throughout Jesus' life on earth, His Father had glorified His own name. Jesus prayed that this would be true, and the Father said in response to the Son's request, "I have both glorified it, and will glorify it again" (12:28).

Jesus as God had divine authority over all flesh and over all whom the Father had given Him. Now on the eve of His death Jesus requested of His Father that even through what those who carried out the dastardly deed at the cross thought was their victory, He would be glorified. And He was.

Jesus' Authority in Prayer, vv. 4–5

Jesus' authority to pray and make the requests He made rested in the Father and in Himself, since He was and is as much God as the Father is God. It is important to note all the personal pronouns He used in these verses when referring to Himself and to His heavenly Father.

Jesus had always glorified God the Father throughout His life on earth. He not only began to do the work He was sent to do; He accomplished it. He finished it. This question comes to mind as we observe Jesus in prayer. Are we doing and completing the work that God wants us to do here on earth? Through all Jesus' words and works as He lived here, He always gave praise and honor to God the Father who had sent Him here. Not long after Jesus prayed this prayer, He said while on the cross, "It is finished" (19:30). The high cost of man's redemption was paid.

What kind of glory was Jesus asking for in this high priestly prayer? It was to be the same glory as His Father possessed. God the Son and God the Father always were of the same divine essence. Both possessed full deity. In the work of the cross which was still future when He prayed, Jesus asked to be glorified along with His Father to the same degree. God the Father did not die on the cross; God the Son did, but He had been given, sent by the Father, to be the one and final Sacrifice for sin.

The glory Jesus possessed before He became man was veiled while He was in His incarnate state. His prayer was that the veil would be removed and His glory displayed as it was before He entered the world. Jesus bore the image of God in the eternities past. While here on earth, He appeared as man. His request was that He might have the glory He had with His father before He was born of Mary.

Personal Applications

This portrait of Jesus painted by John the apostle ought to cause us to think seriously about our prayer life. Some hard questions need to be asked.

What is our approach in prayer like? Do we ever barge into God's presence? We must not ever think prayer and the answer we want is like an entitlement which is owed us. Instead, prayer is a wonderful privilege for the believer. Our prayers should not always be "give me" prayers or "bless" me and others I know and love. Prayer is our way of talking to God. He expects us to be very honest and open with Him but at the same time reverent and submissive to His will, whatever it may be.

Prayer is an important aspect of worship. It is easy to drift into thinking worship can only be done when we sing or meditate at specified times in a church service.. We worship God when we exalt Him, praise Him, extol Him in our minds. We need to remember that when we bow in prayer, we are approaching the King of kings and Lord of lords. We are coming before the God of all the universe, the One who spoke the word and worlds, came into existence.

It will be good for us to also ask ourselves what our appeals, our requests, are to God. Here is a good but hard exercise for you. Try praying without asking God for anything. It is hard, is it not? Why not start praying prayers of thanksgiving? Make a list of things you are thankful for and look at it as you pray.

Prayer should not be an attempt to force God's hand or make him change His mind. Instead, it is more a time, as we are open before God, for us to get close to Him and to see things from His perspective. In other words, to simply worship Him.

Another truth we are reminded of from listening to Jesus pray is so important. It is concerned with the believer's authority in prayer. That is, not what authority do we have as we pray? Rather, we need to remember that we must always come in prayer on the authority of the triune God. Apart from Jesus we have no right to approach God. He is the One and only Mediator between God and man, the Man Christ Jesus (1 Timothy 2:5).

Scripture exhorts believers to pray without ceasing (1 Thessalonians 5:17). This means to pray like a person with a hacking cough. That is, we need to be sincere and persistent in the worship of prayer. Is it not interesting how we parents find it necessary to constantly tell our children to be thankful when people do things for them or give them something? Why is that? Could it be that this is true because we as parents are selfish and self-centered so often. Scripture exhorts God's people over and over again to be thankful, to praise God. Why?

Study Questions

1. Was Jesus worshipping God as He prayed? Do You?

2. Do you think Jesus was teaching His disciples anything about prayer as He prayed? Why?

3. How does this portrait of Jesus affect you and your prayer life?

4. What temptations accompany praying in public?

5. Why is it important for us to pray since God is sovereign?

6. What should be prominent in our prayers?

Praying for His Own

Portrait 25

John 17:6–26

IT MUST have seemed almost too good to be true. Yet they heard Jesus praying with their own ears for them. He had just finished talking to His heavenly Father about Himself and how He wanted the Father to be glorified and Himself as well through His death on the cross. But now Jesus is praying specifically for His eleven disciples. Judas had already departed and was carrying out His plans to betray Jesus.

I cannot help but wonder what the eleven thought when Jesus concluded His high priestly prayer with requests for all who would believe in Him because of the work of the disciples. Had these men ever even thought about their ministry after Jesus would leave them? Probably not, because they expected Him to establish His kingdom in which they would rule and reign with Him.

Indeed it is hard to believe that Jesus, God's only begotten Son, prayed for you and for me, including all who accept Him as their Savior. I am getting convicted about my own prayer habits. Are you? Jesus is God's Son. There never was a time when He did not exist. Why, He even was involved in creating the universe and all that is in it. It would seem He had no need to pray, does it not? We need to remember that Jesus had come into the world to carry out His Father's plan. He had no agenda of His own but was determined to carry out all His Father had planned for Him. As He prayed, He communed with God the Father; He worshipped Him. In this portrait we are going to listen in to His prayer for all who were His and those who would become His in the future. Listen up now as He prays first for the eleven whom He had chosen to be His personal disciples. Try to put yourself in their place right there with Him listening to His prayer.

Prayer for the Disciples, vv. 6–19

As Jesus talked with His Father about these men, He mentioned three specific reasons or purposes for His prayer. We want to give special attention to these. But before we do, let us be sure we note some specifics Jesus used in describing His disciples to His Father.

First, He said these men were given to Him by the Father. They belonged to the Father; they were His in a special sense. God gave them to Jesus, and they kept God's Word (v. 6). What a wonderful verse to help us remember the portrait. Let us make it the key verse. Second, because these men had been with Jesus and worked with Him and for Him, they knew the Father had provided for Jesus all He needed to do His work on earth (v. 7). They came to know and understand that what Jesus taught them was from the Father. They had no doubt that Jesus was sent by God the Father, and they believed in Him fully (v. 8).

Third, Jesus reminded the Father that He was not praying for the world of mankind generally but specifically for those He had given to Jesus (v. 9). It is important to remember that Judas Iscariot was not with Jesus and the disciples any longer, and Jesus did not pray for him, at least not at this time.

Now let us look at the three purposes of Jesus' prayer for His disciples. Jesus stressed that He prayed for these men because they were the Father's and His jointly (v. 10). Jesus had been glorified, praised, exalted in them or through them. So we could say this first reason for Jesus' prayer for the disciples was because of their identity, because of who they were in relation to Jesus.

A second reason why Jesus prayed for His disciples was because of His upcoming absence from them. He would not be physically on planet earth much longer but they would be. And because of the intense hatred of the world for them, they needed supernatural assistance as they would be spreading Jesus' message (v. 11a). While they served with Him for at least three years, they depended fully on Him for all their needs. Jesus did not want them to be as orphans after His ascension back to His Father.

Reason number three in our Lord's purposes for praying for His disciples was that they needed security for their future work (v. 12). Jesus had kept them up to now. Since He would soon be leaving them, He commended them to the Father for their safekeeping. He kept in His name all who were truly His. Jesus guarded them every step of the way. Not one of those who had received Him as their Savior and Israel's Messiah was lost. One did perish but he, "the son of perdition," was not given to Jesus by the Father. Earlier, Jesus said, "one of you is a devil," and He was referring to Judas Iscariot (6:70–71). Judas played the part very well. Perhaps none of the others in the group ever suspected him. Satan entered into Judas as the group gathered in the Upper Room a bit earlier (13:27). It is important to observe that Jesus did not say He had kept all given to Him by the Father except Judas. Rather, He said He had kept them all but "the son of perdition." This expression was a Hebraic one meaning doomed to eternal condemnation.

A fourth clearly stated purpose for Jesus' prayer for the eleven was because of their heavenly citizenship (17:16). These followers of Jesus were not of the world. This means they did not embrace the philosophy of the world. Instead, they were followers of Jesus. He was not of the world and neither were they.

The final reason or purpose for Jesus' prayer for His disciples was because they had been given a high and holy calling or commission. What exactly was that? It was that they were sent into the hostile environment of the world (v. 18). In the world they were to shine as lights. Jesus Himself had been sent by the Father into the world, and now He was sending these disciples into that same antagonistic world. Is that not true of all who have claimed Jesus as their Savior? Indeed it is. We too have the same assignment those men did. How goes that battle, by the way?

Now that we have observed the five reasons or purposes of Jesus' prayer for the disciples, let us notice the four specific petitions for which He prayed.

Jesus was very concerned about the unity the men needed to serve Him most effectively. "Holy Father, " He prayed, "keep them in Thy name . . . that they may be one, even as We are" (v. 11). Interestingly, that address, "Holy Father," is found only here in the Gospels. How appropriate it is here in stark contrast with the wickedness in the world in which the men would be ministering. This was not a request for organizational unity or union. Rather, it was for unity with each other as they served. They each had unique individual gifts and talents, and these must be exercised without jealousy and pride but unitedly to honor God.

Personal fellowship with God was also one of Jesus' requests for the eleven. He desired that His joy would be "made full in them" (v. 13). On the eve of Jesus' crucifixion and promised return back to the Father there was certainly need for comfort This speaks of personal fellowship with God. There is nothing more important for the servant of the Lord and for every believer. Where there is no fellowship with God, there will be no joy. This is more than happiness or lightheartedness. It is more like peacefull calm in the midst of storms. By the same token, where there is not obedience, there will be no fellowship. In other words, joy is dependent upon fellowship, and fellowship is accompanied by obedience. These are all dependent upon intimacy with the Lord Jesus.

The disciples also needed protection from evil and Satan the evil one (v. 15). There would be times when these men would wish to be taken out of the world. But that is not what Jesus asked the Father for. Rather, He prayed that they would be kept from the evil one. Not deliverance from trials and troubles but preservation through is what Jesus prayed for. They, and all of God's people, need to be kept from the evil one because they, like Jesus, are not "of the world" (v. 16).

The fourth request Jesus made for the eleven disciples was the need for them to be set apart or sanctified in truth and unto truth (v. 17). This was not a prayer for their salvation. Each of the eleven had already received Jesus as his only hope of heaven. Jesus Himself in this prayer said He, for their sakes, sanctified Himself (v. 18). Both Jesus and the eleven were set apart to truth. They were set apart for the purpose of God for them.

Prayer for Future Believers, vv. 20–26

Jesus actually prayed for all who would accept Him as the Substitute for their sin from the time of His prayer to the end of time. Is that wonderful or what? After He finished praying for Himself and the eleven disciples with Him, He prayed for you and me. He died for all, but He prayed only for those who would be His children. It is apparently our job to pray for unbelievers to come to faith in the Savior.

For what is it specifically that Jesus prayed for future believers? Two things in particular seem to stand out in His prayer, this portrait, we are now gazing at.

First, He asked God the Father that those who believe in Him through the Word and witness of the disciples might experience a spiritual unity. He asked that they would be one. Earlier in Jesus' prayer for the disciples He requested the same of His Father (v. 11). Spiritual unity is in view here, not organizational unity which the liberal ecumenists are seeking for in our world today.

The kind of unity or oneness Jesus was asking for is clear from what He said as a part of His request. "Even as Thou Father, art in Me, and I in Thee" (v. 21) describes the unity called for. The answer to Jesus' prayer is given in Ephesians 4:4–6. The "unity" is not something man creates by not being concerned about what is believed about the foundational doctrines of the historic Christian faith. It is not an inclusivistic manufactured "unity" at the expense of truth.

There already exists a divine unity undergirding the church which is Christ's body. There is already established a divine unity not created by man. There is one God, one Savior, and one Holy Spirit. All in the family of God have been redeemed by the same blood, have the same Holy Spirit, the same hope, same keeping power, same keeping promises and the same blessed hope. There are realities in answer to Jesus' prayer for us. What we need to do as God's people is to recognize these facts and blessed truths and live accordingly as we behave as brothers and sisters in God's family.

Because we are so prone to sin, we often fail to acknowledge these truths. As a result, the world, those we seek to bring into the family of God, often turn a deaf ear to the salvation God offers.

The second thing Jesus prayed for on our behalf was our security (vv. 24–26). What a wonderful truth that is. Jesus willed, He desired, that all those given to Him by the Father would be with Him forever in heaven. Why was this Jesus' desire? It was so that all the redeemed would see His glory given to Him by the Father before the foundation of the world.

We know, as Jesus knew, that He was always heard by the Father (11:42). We know too that God "remains faithful and cannot deny Himself" (2 Timothy 2:13). We are secure in Him. Both Jesus and the Father hold us in their hands (10:28–29). As God's children, we are to be like salt and light in the world we are in, but we are not supposed to be of it. This means believers are to have a God-centered philosophy of life so they will not advance Satan's anti-God agenda.

Personal Applications

Jesus is our greatest encouragement to prayer. We may not know all we would like to know about prayer, but that we should pray is beyond dispute. Not only do we have His great example in prayer, but we also are encouraged throughout the Bible to worship God in prayer and to bring our needs before Him. He delights in worshipful prayer and prayer for guidance and the necessities of life.

As we pray, we need to approach Him and talk to Him as our best Friend. He knows what our burdens are, the sincerity of our hearts or lack of it, and all our needs; yet He not only invites us to come to Him in prayer but exhorts us to do so .

We have great cause to rejoice in our safety in Jesus. He has promised it and has requested it of His Father. When Satan comes with his doubts and denials, we need to remember what Jesus our Savior has promised in His Word.

Study Questions

1. What was Jesus facing as He prayed this prayer?

2. How does what He faced compare with what we often face when we pray?

3. Do you believe Jesus' prayer for Himself, His disciples, and you was answered?

4. What two things were uppermost in Jesus' prayer for all future believers?

5. Are there steps you can and should take to improve your prayer life? What are these? When do you plan to take that first step?

Rejected, Arrested, and Tried

Portrait 26

John 18:1–19:15

IMAGINE IT! Jesus the Son of God was rejected by people He came to save. He was arrested, tried, and soon after that put to death by those He came to give eternal life.

The arrest came very soon after He prayed His great High Priestly prayer. Jesus was in communion and fellowship with God the Father and had just finished praying for all who would ever come to trust Him as their Substitute.

From the human perspective, everything about His arrest and trials was unjust. It was in the Garden of Gethsemane where Jesus was again in prayer where He was arrested as a result of Judas Iscariot's betraying scheme. John tells us Jesus and His disciples went often to this garden with His disciples which would include Judas.

I cannot help but wonder what went through Judas' mind as he led the soldiers and officers to the very same place he had often been with Jesus. His sin of rejection had hardened his heart to the point that he conspired with the Jewish leaders to lead them where he knew Jesus would be.

All sin has a way of doing that. Usually, it is a gradual thing. Surely Judas had planned ahead of time to betray Jesus. His awful sin did not just come about on the spare of the moment. Even though Judas acted as though he was a true disciple of Jesus and played the part of a true follower, yet behind all the play-acting he never was a true believer.

We want to see in this portrait of Jesus how He was rejected by four individuals and groups. First, notice how Judas carried out his rejection of Jesus.

Rejected by Judas, 18:1–11

As we observe this portrait, we must keep in mind that Jesus was not surprised at what Judas did or what any of the others pictured in this portrait did.

After the foot-washing experience in the Upper Room, Jesus said, "Let us go from here" (14:31). It seems highly likely therefore that He and His disciples left the Upper Room, and His High Priestly prayer was prayed somewhere between where He washed the disciples feet and the Garden of Gethsemane. It could be that Jesus and the eleven went from the Upper Room to the temple before they went to the Gethsemane Garden. We do know that Jesus and the eleven crossed the "ravine of the Kidron" which was not very far from the temple. There in the garden the arrest took place.

Judas knew Jesus would be there because he and the other disciples often went there with Him. Judas came with the Roman cohort along with the officers from the chief priests and Pharisees. They came fully prepared to take Jesus with them. Before they even were close enough to do that, Jesus went to them since He knew they would come and what they planned to do. He asked them a question which He knew the answer to before He asked it. Remember, it was dark and the captors came with lanterns, torches, and weapons.

"Whom do you seek?" Jesus asked them. They said, "We seek Jesus of Nazareth." He said to them and Judas who was standing there with Him, "I am He." They were so overtaken that they stumbled over their own feet as they moved back further away from Jesus and fell to the ground.

As they were getting up and trying to stand up, Jesus asked them again, "Whom do you seek?" and again they said the same thing, "Jesus of Nazareth." His answer was the same with an added word. "If you are looking for Me," He said, "let these go their way" (18:8). Apparently He was referring to the eleven with Him.

Jesus then referred to His prayer for His true disciples of whom He had lost none. They had been given to Him by God the Father. This response by Jesus clearly shows that Judas had never been given to Him by the Father (v. 9).

About that time Peter, who heard all that had been said by the soldiers and Jesus, took out his sword and cut off the right ear of the high priest's slave (v. 10). Most likely Peter was intending to kill the slave. He was a good fisherman but a poor swordsman. Jesus rebuked Peter and restored the slave's ear (v. 11; cf. Luke 11:51). There is a lot in this portrait. Let us observe it carefully.

Rejected by the Officers, 18:12–14

We are not sure exactly how many individuals were involved in the "Roman cohort." It could have involved as many as 600 soldiers some of whom may have been stationed nearby. We do know the "commander" was with those who were led by Judas to the garden. They arrested and bound Jesus and took Him first to Annas. Officers of the Jews who had been sent earlier (7:44–45) but had not succeeded in arresting Jesus were also there with the soldiers.

Annas was the father-in-law of Caiaphas. He had been deposed earlier, but he still carried some weight and influence behind the scenes, so to speak. He was in fact vice president of the Sanhedrin ruling body. Jesus' appearance before this man was followed by two other Jewish trials.

Rejected by Peter, 18:15–27

But before those trials John gives us a picture of Peter and his denial of Jesus (vv. 15–17). Peter was with another unnamed disciple following at some distance as Jesus was before Annas. It is generally agreed that this other disciple was John. All the disciples had forsaken Jesus and fled (Matthew 26:56). Then later, Peter and John came back to the high priest's house where Jesus was being interrogated. John was no doubt able to go into the house because he was known by the high priest (18:16). Peter stayed just outside the door for some time but then went and identified himself, and Peter was also permitted to enter the house at this crucial time.

The slave girl who watched the entrance to Annas' house questioned Peter. "You are not also one of this man's disciples, are you?" she asked. Peter's answer was, "I am not" (v. 17). Some of the other slaves and officers were warming themselves at a charcoal fire they had started. Peter stood close by and joined them. Needless to say, he was at the wrong place with the wrong people at the wrong time. That often is true of us too.

The high priest began to question Jesus about His teaching and His disciples. Without answering directly, Jesus responded by telling him to ask those who heard Him. When Jesus said this, the officer standing close hit Jesus and rebuked Him for speaking to the high priest in that way. In response to the officer Jesus said, "If I have spoken wrongly, bear witness of the wrong; but if rightly, why do you strike Me?" (v. 23).

Annas wanted desperately to get Jesus off his hands. So, he sent Him, still bound, to Caiaphas. Peter, it seems, stayed by the fire and the officers. Again, he was asked the same question which the slave girl had asked him. Peter answered in the same way denying he was one of Jesus' disciples. Once again, therefore, he was rejecting Jesus. Was he really intending to do this?

One of the high priest's slaves who was a relative of the man whose ear Peter had cut off also questioned Peter. The slave was sure he had seen Peter in the garden using his sword on his relative. Again, for the third time Peter denied he was Jesus' disciple. Most likely Peter was really attempting to split the servant's skull but aimed poorly. Then it was as Jesus said, a cock crowed. Try to imagine how Peter felt at that time. How sad it was, despite all his promises to the contrary, Peter denied his Lord. Have you ever done that in one way or another? How did you feel afterwards?

Rejected by Pilate and the Jews, 18:28–19:15

From Annas, Jesus was taken to Caiaphas and from there to the Praetorium early in the morning. This was the Roman headquarters, a barracks of sorts. Since Gentiles occupied the place, it was viewed as unclean by the Jews. For this reason, they would not enter lest they be defiled. How interesting that they did not want to be defiled for the Passover celebration but did not at all mind seeing to it that Jesus was put to death. They were doing some twisted and distorted thinking.

Pilate went outside therefore to Jesus' accusers and murderers and asked them what accusation they had against Jesus. Proud Pontius Pilate was characterized by weakness in contrast to Herod who was characterized by hardness of heart.

John does not include Jesus' appearance before Herod in his account of the trials. Luke does include this (Luke 23:6). It was after Pilate asked Jesus if He was the King of the Jews, to which Jesus gave the affirmative answer, that Pilate heard reference from the accusing crowd to Herod whose jurisdiction Jesus was under, and then he quickly sent Jesus to Herod. Pilate busied himself trying to get Jesus off his hands. History has it that Jesus was on trial before Pilate. But it was really the other way around—Pilate was on trial before Jesus.

Jesus' answer to Pilate's question, "What have you done?" was "My kingdom is not of this world. If My kingdom were of this world, then My servants would be fighting so I would not be handed over to the Jews; but as it is, My kingdom is not of this realm" (vv. 35–36).

What could Jesus have meant by that? Had He not preached "Repent for the kingdom of heaven is at hand"? Did He not send out His disciples and the seventy to preach the same message? His forerunner preached that same message also. But now this message had been totally rejected, Therefore, the nation of Israel through its leaders had crossed the line. The kingdom offer which Jesus gave was now withdrawn. For want of a better word, we say it was postponed. Jesus the Son of God is as good as His word. His earthly kingdom will be instituted in a day still future. From the throne of David in Jerusalem He will yet rule over the whole world with perfect justice and peace for all who submit to His rule.

It has been accurately said that Jesus' trials were before Jews and Romans. There were actually three Jewish trials. There was one before Annas, one before Caiaphas, and one before the Sanhedrin. This last one has been recorded by Matthew in 27:1–2. There were also three Roman trials, one before Pilate, then before Herod, and then back to Pilate. Much about each of these trials was illegal. But that did not seem to matter to the blood-thirsty foes who wanted Him out of the way and out of their lives.

The portrait which John painted of Jesus rejected, arrested, and tried continues through John 19:1–15. At the close of chapter 18 Pilate is interviewing Jesus. He said to Him in the form of a question, "So You are a King?" (18:37). "Yes, I am, Jesus answered. I was born to be a king." Further, Jesus said to Pilate, "I have come into the world to testify to the truth. Everyone who is of the truth hears My voice" (v. 37). It was then Pilate interrupted with, "What is truth?" (v. 38). He then left Jesus and went out to the hostile mob of Jews and told them he could find no fault in Him. But, he said, you Jews have a custom that says someone is to be released for you at the Passover. When Pilate asked them whom he should release to them, Barabbas or Jesus, they screamed saying they wanted Barabbas the robber and not Jesus (v. 40). This key verse should help you think through the rest of this account.

Pilate was at the end of his rope. He had Jesus scourged. This was a flogging with a leather whip that had pieces of either bone or metal or both in it. The Romans used this only for murderers and traitors. Why, you may ask, did Pilate do this? Very likely he did it thinking the Jews would be satisfied with such cruel torture and back off of their demand that Jesus be crucified. No, Pilate still had Jesus on his hands. His scheme did not work.

The soldiers put a crown of thorns on Jesus' head and put a purple robe on Him. They taunted Him and mocked Him, slapping His face. Again, Pilate came out and told the angry mob he could find no fault in Him. Jesus was brought before His accusers again wearing the crown of thorns and purple robe. The chief priests and officers cried out again, "Crucify, crucify." With that, Pilate had his fill. He told the Jews to take Jesus and crucify Him themselves. What did the Jews do then? They quickly reminded Pilate that their law called for His death because He made Himself out to be the Son of God or, in other words, equal with God. That is what Son of God means when referring to Jesus. Scripture does not refer to Jesus as the child of God but the Son of God, meaning He is of the same divine essence as the Father.

Pilate, the Roman governor, became very troubled by what the Jews said. In fact, he became afraid. He went back into the Praetorium and asked Jesus where He was from. Jesus did not answer him. That silence upset Pilate even more. He reminded Jesus that he had the authority to release Him or have Him crucified. Jesus then answered Pilate that he really had absolutely no authority over Him at all unless it would be given to Him by His heavenly Father. This, it seems, further upset Pilate because he again tried to get Jesus released. But it did not work. The crowd only put Pilate in a state of panic by telling him if he released Jesus, he would no longer be a friend of Caesar.

That did it! He brought Jesus out and had Him sit on the judgment seat and said to the Jews, "Behold, your King" (v. 14). They were not impressed. Instead, they screamed at Pilate saying, "Away with Him, crucify Him!" "Shall I crucify your king?" he asked them. Speaking for them all the chief priests said, "We have no king but Caesar" (v. 15). Pilate had exhausted all his options. He handed Jesus over to them to be crucified.

Personal Applications

The closer you and I walk with our Lord in close fellowship with Him, the more likely we are to be rejected by friends and sometimes even family. We will probably not be arrested and tried for being a follower of Jesus as long as we obey the laws of the land.

Being rejected is hard. It can really be upsetting and heartbreaking. Jesus lived a perfectly sinless life and yet He was despised and rejected by some, especially the religious Jews of His day. He did not instruct His disciples to wage any kind of opposition against those who rejected Him. Instead, He challenged them to love their enemies and do good to those who despitefully use them.

When we and our lifestyle are ignored or even obviously rejected, we still need to be kind even to those who are not kind to us. The fruit of the Spirit needs to characterize our lives at all times to all people.

Surely you noticed from this portrait of Jesus that He was also rejected by Peter, one of His disciples. True, it was not the same kind of rejection as from the religionists toward Jesus. But it was a rejection nonetheless. When Peter should have stood tall without any shame for being a close follower of Jesus, he failed miserably. Have you ever found yourself in shoes almost like Peter's? Thankfully God forgave Peter and even used him mightily later. Peter repented with tears for his poor behavior. God will do the same for us. He is so good!

Study Questions

1. How would you characterize Judas Iscariot?

2. Where was Jesus arrested? How did Judas know Jesus would be there?

3. Why, do you suppose, Peter of all people denied that he was a follower of Jesus?

4. How would you summarize Pilate's handling of Jesus and the Jews who brought Jesus to him?

5. Note how many attempts Pilate made to get Jesus off his hands. These are recorded in 18:31, 38, 39; 19:1, 5, 14.

Crucified

Portrait 27

John 19:16–42

Jesus was born of Mary so that He might die as a Substitute for the sins of mankind. Luke, the physician, put it this way, "The Son of Man has come to seek and to save that which was lost" (Luke 19:20). Jesus was obedient to His Father's will even unto death. We must not think Jesus came to earth to die reluctantly or against His will. No, He came to carry out the divine will and plan, and He did so willingly and gladly. Always, He did everything pleasing to God the Father.

Two extremes were demonstrated at the cross. The immensity of God's love was demonstrated on Golgotha's hill that day and so was the enormity of man's sin and guilt. We could say Calvary has two sides, the side of gloom and the side of glory. Or to put it another way, there is man's side and there is God's side.

The side of gloom is seen when we remember that Jesus the sinless One died at the hands of sinful men. When compared to the crime committed at Calvary, all other crimes pale into misdemeanors by comparison. No crime in all the annals of history, both sacred and secular, are even comparable to the crucifixion of Jesus. Think of it! The sinless perfect Lamb of God was put to death by wicked sinful humans.

In addition, the side of gloom is also established by the response of creation itself to the dastardly deed done at Calvary. When Jesus died, the earth quaked and even trembled in anger, as it were. There was darkness for three hours which was as though the heavens were responding in shame at the death of Jesus, the Creator. It was all of creation threatening to swallow up the creatures on it in response to their rejection of Jesus (cf. Matthew 27:45–51). How true it is, the crucifixion of Jesus from the viewpoint of unbelievers was a crime, a tragedy worse than any other ever committed.

But the cross was not an accident which overthrew the sovereign purpose and plan of God. He was not shocked or dismayed when Jesus, His only begotten Son, was put to death any more than He was surprised when Satan sinned and then Adam and Eve. Yes, Jesus was put to death by the wicked, but He was also "delivered by the determined counsel and foreknowledge of God" (Acts 2:23. The prophet Isaiah even wrote that "it pleased the LORD to bruise Him (Isaiah 53:10) in death.

The glory side of the cross reveals the universal and glorious provision which Jesus made for the salvation of sinners. God the Father took Jesus, God the Son, the rejected One, and brought triumph to Himself through the very event men view as a tragedy. In other words, God took the gloom, the sorrow, and turned it into glory, grace, and salvation. The One whom man spit upon and debased God the Father raised from the dead and exalted Him to His own right hand with a name above every other name (Philippians 2:9–11).

Let us walk through chapter 19 of John and see the preparation, execution, and verification of Jesus the crucified.

Preparation for Jesus' Crucifixion, vv. 16–24

Proud Pontius Pilate brought Jesus out to the Jews one last time and said, "Behold your King" (John 19:14). They would have nothing to do with Him and responded accordingly. They said, "Away with Him, away with Him, crucify Him" (v. 15). It was as though he could not believe their response. "Shall I crucify your King?" he asked them. Their answer was clear and very frightening to Pilate. "We have no king but Caesar," they cried out. You might say the Roman governor was at the end of his rope. He had tried and tried to get Jesus off his hands but he could not. Begrudgingly and no doubt fearfully, Pilate handed Jesus over to His accusers to be crucified (v. 16). This short verse is key to everything around it. It sums up everything.

Crucifixion was certainly the most shameful and painful form of death at that time. The one crucified often only died two or three days later. The crucified died of thirst, sheer exposure, unbelievable pain and eventually of asphyxiation. The usual procedure was to nail the victim's hands to the crossbeam. Then the crossbeam was secured to the upright part. The feet were then nailed to the upright. A small piece of wood was secured to the upright for the victim to sit on. To be sure the one crucified was dead, his legs were broken. In the case of Jesus He was already dead when the soldiers came to break His legs.

Jesus carried His cross toward Golgotha until He fell beneath its load. The place was also called the place of a skull probably because the hill resembled a human skull, where He was crucified. Two others were crucified at the same time, one on each side of Jesus. Pilate had a hard time trying to placate and please the angry Jews. They vehemently reacted to the inscription which Pilate had placed on the top of the cross. It read, "JESUS THE NAZARENE, THE KING OF THE JEWS" (V. 19). This inscription was written in three languages—Hebrew, Latin, and Greek.

The chief priests complained and insisted the inscription should read, "He said, I am the King of the Jews." Pilate was defiant and in disgust said, "What I have written, I have written" (v. 22).

The soldiers who were there took Jesus' outer garments and made four parts, one for each soldier. They did the same with Jesus' tunic. They were careful not to tear the tunic. Instead they cast lots to see who would get it. Little did they know they were fulfilling Scripture when they did this (cf. Psalm 22:18).

Execution of Jesus' Crucifixion, vv. 25–30

Be sure to notice in John's portrait the people gathered at the cross. There were the soldiers somewhere close by along with the chief priests and officers. Jesus' mother also and His mother's sister, probably Salome, wife of Zebedee, Mary the wife of Cleophas, and Mary Magdalene were there. This last named Mary was the one Jesus had delivered from seven demons (Luke 8:2). She was from the town of Magdala which was between Capernaum and Tiberias. John, the beloved disciple, was also present. No other friends of Jesus are named. We might ask where the other disciples were at this critical hour. Why were these people there at the cross? Why were not more there, especially among the many Jesus healed?

The soldiers were there because their duty was to be there. The chief priests and Jewish officers were there to satisfy their determination to get rid of Jesus. The few of Jesus' friends were drawn there out of love and devotion to Jesus, no doubt.

Notice too the pronouncements Jesus made while on the cross. John includes three of His last words spoken before He died. "Woman, behold your Son," He said to Mary His mother, and in turn to John He said, "Behold your mother" (vv. 26–27). John is the only one of the Gospel writers to include this twofold word. Interestingly, Mary was not told to care for John and the rest of the disciples. It is the other way around.

At first glance this word of Jesus sounds rather rude to refer to His mother as "woman." However, it was instead a word of respect and endearment, though He no longer had the same relationship with her. She was not a rival in His work. He was the Redeemer; she was not. She, as all others, needed redemption, and Jesus provided it. Jesus' respect and watchcare over His mother should serve as an example to all of us as we relate to our mothers, always, not just on Mother's Day. Indeed this final word to His mother was a word of comfort and compassion from Jesus.

John's second word from Jesus as He was on the cross was, "I am thirsty" (v. 28). This was a word of physical anguish and agony. This was one word with two syllables. Here was the Cocreator of heaven and earth with parched lips. Here was the Lord of glory in need of a drink of water which He had created. Remember too this was the Jesus who earlier had turned water into wine (2:1–11) and the One who had asked the Samaritan woman, "Give Me to drink" (4:7). Jesus asked for a drink as He was dying. Of the seven words which He uttered while on the cross this was the only one that was a cry of pain.

The cry from Jesus becomes more meaningful when we remember what preceded it. There were the mock trials, lashes with the whip laced with sharp pieces of steel, carrying His cross, being nailed to the cross, and the hot scorching sun blazing upon Him. Little wonder that He cried, "I am thirsty." He was fully God and also Man. It was because of His genuine humanity that He thirsted. Earlier, Jesus was offered a stupefying drink intended to release some of the terrible pain (Matthew 27:34). This Jesus refused, but now with His work finished while in a fully conscious state, He asked for a drink. He drank the vinegar-like liquid that they gave to Him.

Immediately after He drank what they gave Him soaked in a sponge made from hyssop, He uttered His word of triumph, "It is finished" (John 19:30). This is one word in New Testament Greek. Without doubt, it is of tremendous importance in the salvation of sinners. What was it that had just been completed? What precisely was Jesus saying was now finished? This word speaks of a tremendous triumph, of victory.

Was the Savior announcing the end of His physical life? Perhaps that was a part of the meaning behind this word. But that hardly needed to be told. Was it not obvious to all who saw Him there that He was about to expire? True, His immense physical suffering was over. Yet there seems to be much more intended by this word. Here are some suggestions with biblical basis of what was finished. Sin's wages were paid. God the Father was fully satisfied with the price Jesus paid for our sins. Proof of this is in the resurrection of Jesus from the dead. The very Lamb of God had paid the full demands human sin created. Jesus made propitiation for the sins of all mankind ever to live. The plan of salvation had all been completed. Jesus paid the full price for our salvation. He provided redemption for all. Also, in His death He reconciled the world to God making sinners saveable.

All of Jesus' accomplishments on the cross were in the nature of a provision. Before any of them bring salvation to anyone, they must be applied to the sinner. That can only be true when Jesus is received as the sinner's Substitute, having died in the sinner's place. All that remains therefore for these provisions to be of benefit is for each one to respond positively to the call of God. That call is for whosoever will, as John says so often in his Gospel.

Verification of Jesus' Death, vv. 31–42

The Passover Sabbath was approaching and the Jews who had demanded Jesus be put to death became terribly concerned about observing the law of the Sabbath. My, how twisted and distorted their thinking was. They did not want Jesus' body to remain on the cross on this Sabbath day. To hasten death, the Jews had the custom of having the legs broken of criminals on a cross. This would make it impossible for the victim to raise himself up so he could breathe and delay his death.

The Jews therefore came again to Pilate and asked that the legs of Jesus and the two crucified with Him be broken. When the soldiers came to Jesus, they did not break His legs because He was already dead. Little did those soldiers realize that Scripture was fulfilled when they did not break Jesus' legs. Prophecy foretold that "He keeps all His bones; not one of them is broken" (Psalm 34:20).

Without naming the soldier, John tells us one of them did pierce Jesus' side. From the wound came both blood and water (John 19:34). This soldier also was fulfilling what was prophesied concerning Jesus. The prophet Zechariah wrote about Jesus' pierced side hundreds of years before He was even born (Zechariah 12:10). John included in this portrait of Jesus the verification of these details of His death fulfilling prophecy (vv. 35–37).

Jesus' death on the cross brought out the worst and the best of some who witnessed it. It brought out the worst from the Jewish leaders and the best from two of Jesus' secret followers. In striking contrast to the hostile behavior of the rulers of the Jews, we see the friendly and loving behavior of Joseph of Arimathea and Nicodemus. Joseph went to Pilate and asked for Jesus' body, obviously to prepare it for burial. Nicodemus, who had come to Jesus earlier and at night for fear of the Jews, joined Joseph of Arimathea bringing a sizeable amount of myrrh and aloes to prepare the body for burial.

Have you ever wondered what these two men thought about as they prepared to bury Jesus' body? Perhaps they regretted their secrecy thinking if they had only made their view of Jesus known, maybe He would have been spared death on a cross. Many thoughts and questions must have raced through their minds as they made Jesus' body ready for burial.

Preparation of bodies for burial in that day and time took time and effort. First, the body was washed, straightened out, and then wrapped in large bandages. These were like sheets of cloth wrapped from the armpits to the ankles. Gummy spices were placed between the cloth. The spices decayed and dried the body making the cloth stiff. Do you remember Jesus' word to those present when He raised Lazarus from the dead? He said to them, "Unbind him and let him go" (10:44).

These two one-time secret followers then took the body of Jesus and buried it. Close by the place where Jesus was crucified there was a garden and in it a new tomb, very likely this was the place now called Gordon's Calvary. Matthew tells us in his account that this tomb belonged to Joseph of Arimathea (Matthew 27:59–60). We must remember that in those days bodies were not buried under ground as they usually are today. Instead, they were placed on elevated surfaces and above ground and the entrance was sealed by stones.

In the next portrait of Jesus we will see the hugh stone at the entrance rolled away and the tomb empty. Jesus was raised from the dead, triumphant over death, hell, and the grave.

Personal Applications

Is there anything more wonderful than that Jesus died for you? No, there most certainly is not. Try to imagine yourself among those gathered at the foot of the cross. Which side do you suppose you would have been on? Would you have been siding with the majority who were there or with the minority?

The Bible teaches very clearly that Jesus satisfied every demand of the offended righteousness of God because of man's sin. He was the sinless Son of God paying the full payment for man the sinner. No more sacrifices need be made for sin, not by God or man. The divine work of redemption is finished. When Jesus died, He was both the Sacrifice and the Sacrificer.

Since the perfect sacrifice for sin has been made by the sinless Savior, nothing man can do can earn favor with God. To try to add anything to Jesus' finished work is an insult to God. He paid it all. If we could add even a tiny bit to what He has done would mean we would be sure of heaven because of Jesus plus some feeble effort on our part.

When Jesus alone is received by faith as the Substitute for our sins, all He accomplished on that cross becomes the believers'. Think of being invited by the President of the United States of America to join him, his family, and other honored guests for dinner at the White House. After the meal, as you leave, you shake his hand and tell him how much you enjoyed the evening. As you shake his hand, you slip him a five dollar bill and tell him you want to help pay for the evening. What a ridiculous and embarrassing thing that would be. It is even worse to try to add your baptism, church membership, or good works to the finished work of Jesus on the cross.

Study Questions

1. How significant is it that some of the things done at the cross were fulfillments of Scripture?

2. Who were the enemies of Jesus present when He died?

3. Who were the friends of Jesus present when He died?

4. What is revealed about the Jews who wanted to be sure they did not violate the Sabbath law?

5. With whom do you plan to share the true meaning and purpose of Christ's death this week?

Raised from the Dead

Portrait 28

John 20

J ESUS' RESURRECTION from the dead is an integral part of the gospel
message. The apostle Paul made that abundantly clear in his letter to
the Christians at Corinth. In his description of the content of the gospel
message which he preached the resurrection of Jesus was prominent. That
gospel centered in Christ's death and resurrection (1 Corinthians 15:1–4).
In his Epistle to the Romans, Paul gave the same emphasis: He was "delivered over because of our transgressions and was raised because of our
justification" (Romans 4:25).

Peter, on the Day of Pentecost, also placed great stress upon the resurrection of Jesus. To the Israelites gathered on that occasion he said of Jesus,
"God raised Him up again, putting an end to the agony of death, since it
was impossible for Him to be held in its power" (Acts 2:24). And again
Peter said, "The God of our fathers raised up Jesus, whom you had put to
death by hanging Him on a cross" (5:30). He even gave the same emphasis
to the Gentiles: "God raised Him up on the third day and granted that He
become visible" (10:40).

Each of the human writers of the first four books of the New
Testament include extended accounts of the resurrection of Jesus from the
dead (Matthew 28:1–16; Mark 16:1–20; Luke 24:1–53 and, of course,
John 20:1–31). None of these accounts include all the same material. Each
writer wrote with a specific purpose in mind for writing his Gospel as God
the Holy Spirit guided him. The resurrection accounts do not contradict
each other. Rather, they supplement each other. We need all of them for
the full story that God wanted us to have.

As John painted his portrait of the resurrected Jesus, he emphasized
two major things: the material evidence and the personal evidence for
Jesus' resurrection. Let us look together at these fascinating evidences.

The Material Evidence of Jesus' Resurrection, vv. 1–10

Mary Magdalene witnessed Jesus' death and was the first one to go to His tomb and find it empty. Mary Magdalene out of whom Jesus had cast seven demons (Mark 16:9) came to the tomb very early in the morning while it was still dark. She seems to have been a leader or outspoken person among three other women. These three would be Mary the mother of James, Salome, and Joanna (Mark 16:1 and Luke 24:10).

Mary Magdalene apparently came to the tomb before the other three women came. She could have done this to check out the scene ahead of time as a leader would often do, especially one so devoted to Jesus because of all He had done for her. The important thing to note is that she found the tomb without the body of Jesus; it was empty except for His grave clothes. These she may not even have observed.

Did Mary Magdalene actually look inside the tomb on this occasion? We do not know for sure. Maybe she saw the huge stone rolled away from the tomb's entrance and concluded that Jesus' body had been stolen. She ran to tell Peter and another disciple, probably John, what she witnessed. These two disciples then ran to the burial place. The disciple with Peter outran him and got there first. He stared into the tomb and saw "the linen wrappings lying there" (v. 5). When Peter arrived, he, as might be expected of him, burst into the tomb and witnessed the same thing. When the disciple with Peter saw what Peter saw from the opening, he also went inside.

So the stone was rolled away from the entrance to the tomb, and the graveclothes were there. They were not just scattered about but were still in tact and undisturbed but without the body of Jesus. The Jews in that day and time did not prepare a dead body as is done today. Without embalming the body, it was wrapped tightly with linen cloth. These were anointed with an ointment of spices. The body was covered from head to toe. A covering was placed over the head. This procedure of preparing the body created a cocoon-like appearance. What Peter and the other disciple saw as they peered into the tomb and then saw closeup was an empty shell without Jesus' body in it.

How did the huge stone get moved away? What happened to the body inside the burial wrappings? There was no evidence of stealing the body. How did Jesus' body get out of the wrappings without disturbing them? There is only one plausible answer to these questions. Miraculously, Jesus arose from the dead and from the grave. Supernaturally, the stone was rolled away by an angel from the Lord (Matthew 28:2). The tomb was empty of the body of Jesus. He arose from the dead, just as He said He would.

All of these who came to the tomb and saw only the grave clothes but not the body of Jesus inside were slow to believe. They did not understand what Jesus had told them before about His resurrection. Lest we become too critical of these friends and followers of Jesus, we need to ask ourselves the question, "Would I have believed if I had witnessed what they did?"

The two disciples "went home" after what they saw. That seems strange, does it not? Why would they do that? You would think they would spread the news far and wide. But they did not. They went "to their own homes" (20:10). Could it be that they were afraid they might be falsely accused by the authorities? Or maybe they were so puzzled over all that happened in the last few days that they needed time to think it all through, to meditate. After all, the open empty tomb without Jesus' body with the cocoon-like form still there certainly must have brought to mind some of the things Jesus had said about His body as a temple which would be destroyed but which He would raise up in three days (John 2:19).

The Personal Evidence of Jesus' Resurrection, vv. 11–31

Did you know that the New Testament records a large number of post-resurrection appearances of Jesus? He appeared to individuals, small groups, and a large group. The chart below lists these appearances along with the Scripture where they are recorded.

Post Resurrection Appearances of Christ

To Individuals

1. Mary Magdalene
2. Peter (1 Corinthians 15:5)
3. James (1 Corinthians 15:7)
4. Stephen at his stoning (Acts 7:55–60)
5. Paul at his conversion (Acts 9:3–8)
6. Paul at Corinth (Acts 18:9–10)
7. Paul in the temple (Acts 22:17–21)
8. Paul Later in Jerusalem (Acts 23:11)
9. Paul on another occasion (2 Corinthians 12:1–4)
10. John on Patmos (Revelation 1)

To Small Groups

1. Women returning from tomb (Matthew 28:8–10)
2. Cleopas and a friend (Mark 16:12)
3. Ten disciples in Jerusalem (John 20:19–250
4. Eleven disciples (John 20:26–31)
5. Seven disciples in Galilee (John 21:1–25)
6. Apostles on Mount of Olives (Acts 1:6–12)

To A Large Group

Apostles and more than 500 brethren (Matthew 28:16–20)

Now look with me at John's portrait of Jesus as He appears to Mary Magdalene in verses 11 through 18. As Mary stood there crying at Jesus' tomb, she stooped down and took a quick peek inside. She saw two angels, one where Jesus' head would have been and the other where His feet would have been. They were both dressed in white. They asked her why she was crying. She answered them with, "Because they have taken away my Lord, and I do not know where they have laid Him" (v. 13). Mary then turned away from the tomb and the two angels inside and saw someone else standing outside the tomb. She did not know it was Jesus.

We must remember that the last time she had seen Jesus, He was so disfigured that He hardly looked like He did before He was put on the cross. She knew too that His body had been placed in the borrowed tomb of Joseph of Arimathea. It was also early in the morning and her eyes were filled with tears.

Jesus then asked Mary why she was weeping and whom she was looking for. He, of course, knew the answer to both of these questions. She thought the gardener was talking to her. Without attempting to answer the questions asked her, she begged Jesus, without knowing He was there, to tell her where the body was so she could go and care for it.

Then it was that Jesus said to her, "Mary" (v. 16). All of us like to be called by our name. When Mary heard her name from this stranger, she finally recognized she was talking to Jesus, not a gardener. She was shocked and responded with, "Rabboni" or teacher. Mary then reached out to Jesus and apparently embraced Him indicating she did not ever want Him out of her sight again. We know that because of Jesus' response to her. He said to her, "Stop clinging to Me" (v. 17). He had others to visit in His resurrected body. He must not be delayed. And, furthermore, now that He had been raised from the dead, He had a whole new relationship with those in their natural bodies. Mary also had urgent work to do. She was to go to the "brethren" and tell them she had seen and talked with Jesus (v. 18).

It was Sunday morning when Jesus appeared to Mary. That same evening Jesus appeared to His disciples. They were behind closed doors for fear of the Jews, but He suddenly stood before them. How shocked they must have been. I wonder how long He stood there in their midst before He said, "Peace be with you" (v. 19). They could not believe their eyes. There He was. They must have suddenly remembered how He told them He would be put to death and raised from the dead.

To be sure all those present would have no doubt about His identity, He "showed them both His hands and His side." They all suddenly had a praise service. They overflowed with joy. Their fear turned into praise as they fellowshipped with Jesus their Lord. Again, He put the disciples at ease with His "Peace be with you" (v. 21).

Jesus was going to give the disciples great authority along with great responsibility. Before doing that, He said to them, "Receive the Holy Spirit" (v. 22). This was a reminder to these men of what Jesus had told them before He went to the cross. You may remember that there in the Upper Room He told them about His upcoming death and that He would return back to the Father who had sent Him. In His place the Holy Spirit, the Comforter, would come and continue what Jesus had done on the earth. The instruction to receive the Holy Spirit here was with a view to the day of Pentecost after Jesus' ascension back to the Father.

The authority and responsibility that the disciples were given concerned their commission to proclaim the gospel message. If they would do this, those who responded positively would have their sins remitted. Those who did not would retain their sin and the consequences of it. We have the same responsibility today. If we who have received Jesus as our Savior give forth the gospel message, those who receive it will have their sins remitted, and those who do not receive it retain their sin (v. 23).

Thomas was not present when Jesus made His first appearance to the eleven disciples. Those who were in that room behind closed doors told Thomas they had seen the resurrected Jesus. Surely, they also told him what Jesus had said to them and How He showed them His hands and side to verify who He was.

Thomas was from the show-me state. I will not believe, He said, until I can put my hands in the nail prints and my finger into where the nails were. Eight days later Jesus appeared again before the disciples and Thomas was there. The eleven had again secretly gathered in a room and closed the doors. Thomas was there this time. "Peace be with you" (v. 26),

Jesus said to them all. He then called to Thomas to come to Him and put his finger into His nail-scared hand and his hand in His side just as Thomas had insisted he needed before he would believe.

Thomas responded to the invitation and did as Jesus told him to do. Without any further delay, he responded with, "My Lord and my God" (v. 28). He used two of the names in the Old Testament. They were *Jehovah* and *Elohim*, the God of creation. Jesus commended Thomas but also reminded him of those who believed before they could see the evidence for their faith.

John the apostle made it clear that he recorded only those signs or miracles which best suited his purpose but that many more could have been included. The Spirit of God led John to use the ones he did so that people everywhere in the world may believe in Jesus as their Savior and have eternal life.

Personal Applications

It is hard to even think about Jesus' resurrection from the dead without being reminded of the apostle Paul's account of it. He wrote to Christians in the city of Corinth. Those believers were being bombarded with some false teaching. They were being told by some among them that "there is no resurrection of the dead" (1 Corinthians 15:12).

Quickly and forcefully the apostle reminded those believers that if there is no resurrection of the dead, it follows that Jesus was not raised from the dead. And if that is true, all of his preaching and teaching is without any merit and so was their faith without merit. And what is more, all who teach that Jesus was raised from the dead are false teachers about God. Without Jesus' resurrection, there is no hope at all for anyone. Can you see from this how indispensable and important Jesus' resurrection really is?

The apostle John certainly believed Jesus really died and really arose from the grave bodily. There was absolutely no doubt in his mind about that. For the believer, the resurrection of Jesus is proof that God the Father accepted the substitutionary death of Jesus. It shows He is completely satisfied with what Jesus accomplished on the cross. Jesus' resurrection is an indispensable part of the gospel message. He died and was raised from the dead according to the Scriptures (1 Corinthians 15:3–4).

Because Jesus arose from the grave, you and I as God's children have hope beyond the grave. Death does not end it all. Our own future resurrection is based on His resurrection. Apart from it, we have absolutely no hope whatsoever. We are of humans most miserable without His resurrection.

Study Questions

1. What material evidence did John include in his portrait of Jesus being raised from the dead?

2. In John's account who was first to come to the empty tomb?

3. What did this person do after looking in the tomb?

4. Would you say you as a believer are living in the power of the resurrection?

5. What suggestions do you have concerning how the resurrection of Jesus is of help to you on a daily basis?

Calling for Followers

Portrait 29

John 21

JOHN'S PURPOSE in giving the portraits of Jesus which we have studied was to show that He came to seek and save those who are lost. The apostle had another purpose in mind also. Those who came to faith in Jesus as their Savior are called upon to be His followers, to reproduce themselves.

After His resurrection from the grave Jesus appeared to a number of individuals. Sometimes He presented Himself to single individuals, other times to small groups, and one to a large company of people. We illustrated this in the last portrait of Jesus. Each time He appeared after His resurrection, it was to verify that He was all He claimed to be—the very Son of God alive from the dead.

Jesus had already appeared to His disciples when Thomas was absent (20:19–25). Eight days later He appeared again when Thomas was present (vv. 26–31). Now sometime later He appeared again to seven of the disciples in Galilee (21:1–25). They were on the Sea of Galilee having fished all night without catching even a minnow. Though they did not at first recognize Him, Jesus stood on the shore.

This portrait of Jesus calling for followers appears almost as a postlude to John's book. In the portrait before this one he summarized all he had written up to that point. He said there were many other signs and wonders Jesus had given which he did not include in his book. But the ones he did include were written so that people would believe that Jesus was the Messiah, the Son of God (20:30–31).

The record of this last portrait is just as inspired as all the other ones before it. In this portrait Jesus "manifested Himself" (v. 1). Twice, this expression appears in the same verse. This means His purpose in appearing was not just to show He arose from the grave. Included in that purpose He also wanted to challenge these seven to not just know about Him but to know Him and serve Him.

Look closely at this portrait with me and notice how Jesus invites His own to serve Him, motivates them for service, and calls for their dedication for service.

Invitation to Service, vv. 1–14

The Sea of Tiberias is also called the Sea of Galilee. Out on that sea in a boat were seven men. They were Simon Peter, Thomas, Nathanael, James and John (James and John called sons of Zebedee here), and two unnamed disciples. They had fished all night and had caught nothing. We must remember these were not novices at the art of fishing. Several of them made their living by fishing. What had happened? Was it by accident that they caught nothing? I think not. Neither their failure or their great success later were accidental.

Let us go back to the start of this whole scenario. Peter was the one who headed up this fishing expedition. Keep in mind he was one of three ring leaders among the disciples, James and John being the other two. Remember too it was Peter who before Jesus crucifixion said to Jesus, "Even though all may fall away because of You, I will never fall away" (Matthew 26:33). Not long after that, he denied three times that he even knew Jesus.

Here in our portrait of Jesus, Peter announces he is going fishing (v. 3). On the surface that sounds innocent enough, does it not? It is not sin to fish. Peter was a fisherman by trade when Jesus called him to be His disciple. That call did not mean he must never fish again.

What is so very important about this statement of fact from Peter is that he used the Greek language of the day in a way that indicates he was quitting the ministry Jesus had called him to and was returning to his old profession of fishing. The tense of the verb which he used tells us he was not going fishing to get some rest and relaxation. No, I gather he was saying, "I quit, I'm going back to what I know and do best–fishing." Peter probably came to this conclusion out of frustration, confusion, and dissatisfaction with himself and his recent behavior.

It appears that very quickly after he made his intention known, the six men with him said to their leader, "We will also come with you" (v. 3). They must have only needed his encouragement to also throw in the proverbial towel, to quit. Here is a reminder to each of us to remember that our language and/or our performance often affects others. It is so important to not forget we are being watched and followed by others around us. We influence others, not just by what we say or fail to say, but also by our behavior.

Earlier in the morning as the new day was "breaking" (v. 4), Jesus was standing on the shore looking out over the water toward the disciples. They did not recognize who it was on the shore line. We cannot help but wonder why they did not know it was Jesus. After all, they had been with Him day and night for about three years. Perhaps it was still somewhat dark and they were so beside themselves because of their failure at their own trade. Also, they were still about 150 yards from the shore.

Jesus called out to them and asked them a question to which He already knew the answer. "Children, you do not have any fish, do you?" He asked them. It was a bit unusual to call His disciples "children." In fact, this was the only time He addressed them or spoke of them in this way. The term He used reminded them that they still needed His instruction. It was a way of letting them know He was going to teach them. The seven renegade preachers in the boat who had come to the end of themselves knew very well what He meant by the word "children." The answer they gave to His question was a rather abrupt "no." It must have been very hard for them to admit their failure to this "stranger" on the shore.

The instruction Jesus gave His discouraged and defeated disciples was contrary to what was normally done by fishermen. Keep in mind they still did not know or at least were not sure who it was giving them this instruction. But I suppose after you have tried all night to catch fish and have come up emptyhanded it is worth trying most anything. Jesus told them to cast their net on the righthand side of the boat. It was customary to put the net on the left side. There is no recorded response from the men. They simply, and it appears immediately, did as they were told. They caught so many fish that they could not even bring in the net. It was too heavy.

After they had done as Jesus told them, John leaned over and said to Peter, "It is the Lord" (v. 7). That was all impetuous Peter needed to hear. Immediately, he put on his outer garment. He was not nude in the boat but was "stripped for work" meaning he was not wearing street clothes.

Why did Peter put on this "outer garment" before he jumped into the water? Most likely, he was following a Jewish custom which said offering a greeting to someone was a religious act, and therefore he needed to be fully clothed. Obviously, Peter fully intended to be the first to greet Jesus and in fact he was. He must have had a change of heart as a result of his failures and Jesus' coming to him and the others despite their sin. That was a display of Jesus' grace, His favor, to the undeserving. Soon after Peter greeted Jesus on the shore, those who were with him in the boat also arrived.

The seven disciples who most likely had decided to quit being Jesus' disciples and go back to their old fishing trade were greeted on the shore by Jesus with a breakfast He had prepared for them. They added some of their fish and had a meal that morning with Jesus. I wonder what they talked about with Him and among themselves?

It appears that Peter counted the fish in their net, all 153 of them. The net was so overloaded that it tore. Not one of the seven quitters dared ask Jesus who He was because they knew. Jesus served the breakfast to the men and revealed Himself to them. John identifies this post-resurrection appearance of Jesus as His third one.

Motivation for Service, vv. 15–17

Jesus had given these disciples a mandate. They were to go into all the world proclaiming His message. He told them, "Go therefore and make disciples of all the nations, baptizing them in the name of the Father and the Son and the Holy Spirit, teaching them to observe all that I commanded you" (Matthew 28:19–20). If they were running away from God, they were certainly not intending to carry out this commission.

After breakfast, Jesus got to the source of the problem. Taking Peter, the ring leader, aside, Jesus questioned him about his love for Him. The very fact that Jesus went to Peter, reached out to him, shows His grace. In tenderness Jesus asked Peter three times about his love for Him (vv. 15–17).

Jesus addressed Peter as "Simon, son of John" (v. 15) three times. This was the name he had before he became a disciple of Jesus. This seems significant in that He had given the name Cephas to him earlier (1:42). Why then revert to Peter's pre-disciple name? Perhaps it was because of the way Peter had been behaving before this incident.

From the English record of the conversation between Jesus and Peter, it appears that Jesus asked the same question and got the same answer from Peter. But that is not the case. Two different words for love are used in the account. The first two times Jesus used the strong word for love which connotes a sacrificial love. In Peter's answers he did not use the same word Jesus used in His question. The word Peter used in his response was something equivalent to the English word "like." Peter did have fondness for Jesus but that was not what Jesus was asking for. Jesus was looking for a much deeper love. In His third question Jesus used the same word Peter had used in his responses to the two earlier questions which he asked Him. Peter's response was the same because he used the same word he had used the other two times the question was asked. In other words, Peter in all honesty could not bring himself to have the kind of love Jesus was looking for. He really did not love Jesus any more than he loved to fish. Interestingly, after each of the three questions Jesus gave Peter a command with a slightly different emphasis, "Tend my lambs" (v. 15), "shepherd My sheep" (v. 16) and "Tend my lambs" (v. 17).

Dedication for Service, vv. 18–25

Jesus continued with His conversation to Peter. The other six disciples were closeby. What they heard, if anything, of what Jesus was saying to Peter, we do not know. Peter did need to know that the sheep he was to care for belonged to Jesus, not to him. He along with the other disciples were undershepherds. Jesus alone was the chief Shepherd.

In addition to the challenge which Jesus gave to Peter He also reminded him of the cross he would be called upon to bear. Jesus predicted that Peter would die as a martyr. Peter understood what Jesus meant when He told him he would. When he grew older, He would "stretch out" his hands and be girded by someone else. He would be taken where he would not wish to go (v. 18). The apostle John said what Jesus told Peter was a picture and prediction of how he would die (v. 19). History records that he did die by crucifixion upside down on a cross.

"Follow Me" (v. 9), Jesus said to Peter. This command was in keeping with what follows when Peter asked how his friend John would die. Jesus mildly rebuked Peter because he seemed more concerned about his fellow disciple's future than he was about Jesus' command to follow Him. So, again Jesus told Peter, "You follow Me" (v. 22). These last three words of this verse set for the thrust of the entire chapter. It is, therefore, the key verse.

Personal Applications

All service for the Lord and to the Lord is very important. From God's perspective there are no little people in the family of God. By that I mean no task done for the glory of God is insignificant. Being a member of the hospitality committee or on the janitorial staff is just as much service for God, if done for His glory, as preaching God's Word or shepherding His sheep is.

Jesus invites all who have accepted Him as their Savior to serve Him. He does this not so we will be sure of heaven or so we will not lose the eternal life He gave us. Rather, He wants us all to get off of the grandstand and get on the stage, as it were, using the talents and gifts He has given us.

Just as Jesus' disciples were to be motivated by the love of Jesus for them and their love for Him, so we should be moved to serve our Lord. Always all of us need to be focused on Jesus. When we have our eyes on ourselves or on others, we will not do well in our Christian walk. Scripture exhorts us over and over again to fix "our eyes on Jesus, the author and perfecter of faith" (Hebrews 12:2).

Study Questions

1. Who first expressed the idea of going fishing in this portrait?

2. Who agreed with him to do the same thing?

3. What should be our primary motive for serving God?

4. How are you serving God?

5. Why do you do what you are doing for God?

CPSIA information can be obtained
at www.ICGtesting.com
Printed in the USA
LVHW051025191221
706635LV00012B/1223